BLAIRSVILLE SENIOR HIGH SCHOOL
BLAIRSVILLE, PENNA.

✮✮✮✮✮✮✮✮✮✮✮✮✮✮✮✮✮

BASEBALL
SUPERSTARS

Hank Aaron

✮✮✮✮✮✮✮✮✮✮✮✮✮✮✮✮✮

✷✷✷✷✷✷✷✷✷✷✷✷✷✷✷✷✷✷

Hank Aaron

Johnny Damon

Derek Jeter

Albert Pujols

Jackie Robinson

Ichiro Suzuki

✷✷✷✷✷✷✷✷✷✷✷✷✷✷✷✷✷✷

BASEBALL SUPERSTARS

Hank Aaron

J. Poolos

☑ Checkmark Books

An imprint of Infobase Publishing

For Helena, who swings for the fence

HANK AARON

Checkmark Books
An imprint of Infobase Publishing
132 West 31st Street
New York, NY 10001

Library of Congress Cataloging-in-Publication Data
Poolos, Jamie.
  Hank Aaron / J. Poolos.
    p. cm. — (Baseball superstars)
  Includes bibliographical references and index.
  ISBN-13: 978-0-7910-9536-2 (hardcover)
  ISBN-10: 0-7910-9536-3 (hardcover)
  ISBN: 978-0-7910-9844-8 (pbk)
  1. Aaron, Hank, 1934- 2. Baseball players—United States—Biography. 3. African American baseball players—Biography. I. Title. II. Series.

  GV865.A25P66 2007
  796.357092—dc22
  [B]

                        2007005916

Checkmark books are available at special discounts when purchased in bulk quantities for businesses, associations, institutions, or sales promotions. Please call our Special Sales Department in New York at (212) 967-8800 or (800) 322-8755.

You can find Chelsea House on the World Wide Web at http://www.chelseahouse.com

Series design by Erik Lindstrom
Cover design by Ben Peterson

Printed in the United States of America

Bang EJB 10 9 8 7 6 5 4 3 2 1

This book is printed on acid-free paper.

All links and Web addresses were checked and verified to be correct at the time of publication. Because of the dynamic nature of the Web, some addresses and links may have changed since publication and may no longer be valid.

CONTENTS

1

The Birth
of a Legend

There is no greater feeling in sports than the one a player gets when his teammates are genuinely excited over one of his own personal accomplishments—excited just to be his teammate. What I remember is that everybody was right there celebrating with me, as if my record was their record, too. A player can't ask for any more than that.

—Hank Aaron, *I Had a Hammer: The Hank Aaron Story*

At first glance, Hank Aaron's story is that of a baseball player who broke one of the most coveted records in the sport: Babe Ruth's long-held mark of 714 career home runs. But it is really the story of an important period in the history of the United States, a period that marked the emergence of racial equality in "America's pastime" and, if not the end of bigotry in baseball, certainly the most significant step forward for black athletes in any sport. For it was during the course of Aaron's career that Major League Baseball teams were at last allowed to add black players to their rosters, changing the face of the game, and of American culture in general, forever.

It was between the white lines of the baseball diamond in the 1950s that African Americans, as players, were permitted to mingle with whites on a more-or-less equal basis. Blacks played on the same ball fields with whites. They traveled to and from games on the same buses, and they suited up in the same locker rooms. At the time, similar occurrences were unheard of in mainstream culture.

Although the laws of segregation were less in force in the Northern states, interaction between the races remained nearly as limited there as in the South. Black people were regarded as second-class citizens in much of the United States. In the South, African Americans were segregated, or separated, from whites, in basic and profound ways. For example, as a rule, if a black man wanted to eat lunch at a restaurant that allowed African Americans (and many of them did not), he entered through the back door. Black people drank from separate drinking fountains than white people. Buses had "white-only" seating toward the front and middle, while blacks sat in a designated section in the back.

As a general rule, individuals of each race came together only when one worked for the other. In the South, black nannies, maids, laborers, and farmers may have built relationships with their white bosses; otherwise, a black person did not go out of his or her way to speak to a white person unless they were spoken to first.

This is not to say that healthy relationships between black and white individuals did not occur. Such relationships were common. But even among the vast majority of racially tolerant Americans—blacks and whites—there was an acceptance of order: whites were citizens, and blacks served them. The opportunity for blacks to enjoy successful lives was limited.

Hank Aaron looks up toward the camera in this portrait taken in 1957 in Milwaukee. That year, Aaron won the National League's Most Valuable Player award. During the 1950s, African Americans were treated as second-class citizens across much of the United States, suffering segregation in many public places. On the baseball diamond, though, racial equality was beginning to emerge.

They lived in the poor neighborhoods, had the dirty jobs, and wore the secondhand clothes. Because black children attended second-rate public schools, the future was no brighter than the present. With such obstacles, it was thought that black men were not destined for greatness.

Hank Aaron rose above racism and bigotry to become a hero. He defined greatness in his generation with his bat and with his inner strength. He rose from an anonymous Negro League ballplayer to a star in the major leagues, though one who was still a target of racism. Through this transformation, Aaron persevered to become a national symbol of triumph in the face of true adversity.

During the Great Depression, which began in 1929 and lasted through much of the 1930s, a black man living in the Deep South did all he could just to survive. Times were hard, particularly for the people of Mobile, Alabama, where the once-thriving cotton industry that had been the staple of the state's economy was in rapid decline. Jobs for laborers were in short supply.

Back then, 30 years before the famous March on Washington, the day Martin Luther King, Jr., delivered his monumental "I Have a Dream" speech, African Americans were denied the basic opportunities typically enjoyed by whites, like the right to vote. Thirty years before the passage of the Civil Rights Act of 1964, which prohibited discrimination in public places, in government, and in employment, there were no black players in Major League Baseball. Thirty years before these events, a man who rewrote history was born.

ROOTS IN MOBILE

Hank's father, Herbert Aaron, moved his young wife, Estella, to Mobile, Alabama, in the late 1920s, just before the Great Depression. At the time, Mobile was a small, quiet city of about 80,000 people. Unlike many Southern cities, which clung to old-fashioned values, Mobile was relatively progressive and forward thinking. In part, these qualities were due to the city's very identity: Mobile was a seaport town, and as a hub for transportation and shipping, it was a rather worldly place, at least in comparison with some of the South's more isolated rural areas.

In terms of racism, according to Hank Aaron's autobiography, *I Had a Hammer*, progressive politicians in Mobile spoke of equal rights between blacks and whites long before civil rights became a popular cause. A local chapter of the NAACP was started in the 1930s. Public libraries in Mobile opened their doors to black people while, across most of the South, African Americans were not even encouraged to learn to read. Make no mistake, however: Racism and all that came with it were nothing short of normal in Mobile.

Herbert and Estella Aaron came to Mobile in the wave of rural African Americans who moved there to look for work. Herbert Aaron moved his family into a mostly black neighborhood called Down the Bay and began to scrape out a living in the shipyards. Times were tough for everyone. The Depression brought waves of layoffs, and Herbert struggled to find steady work. For a while, Estella worked as a housekeeper and cleaning woman. In fact, most of the African Americans who migrated to Mobile during the Depression found work not in Alabama's cotton industry but as maids, nannies, and cooks in the homes of white people. It was not long, though, before Estella turned her attention away from domestic work and toward the family she would raise.

Henry Louis Aaron, Herbert and Estella Aaron's third child, was born on February 5, 1934. "Hank," as he would later be called, came into the world one day before baseball great Babe Ruth's thirty-ninth birthday. At the time, the Aarons lived in an apartment on Wilkinson Street in Down the Bay and would spend the next several years there. As World War II began, more and more people came to Mobile to work in the shipyard. By now the Aarons had six children, and they were outgrowing their apartment. In 1942, Herbert and Estella decided it was time to find their family a home with more room.

Herbert Aaron paid $110 for two vacant lots on Edwards Street in the nearby village of Toulminville, where many of Mobile's black families were moving to escape the overcrowded city. There, Herbert planned to build his family a home. The building next to the Wilkinson Street apartment had recently been torn down, and Herbert acquired the lumber and hired a pair of carpenters to build a house.

The new house had six rooms, which was several more than the Aaron family had ever had. The house had no lights and no windows to let in light, but the Aarons had no rent or mortgage to pay either, so no one complained.

"We were a proud family because the way we saw it, the only people who owned their own homes were rich folks and Aarons," Hank Aaron recounted in *I Had a Hammer*. The new home, though, presented plenty of challenges. Herbert continued to gather building materials wherever he found them and over time put the finishing touches on the home.

Toulminville provided a quiet, rural setting for the Aarons. The village was known for its groves of oak trees and for the county fair organized by the village's founder, General Theophilus Toulmin. The folks there had cows, chickens, and hogs. And watermelon and blackberry patches were sprinkled among the fields of corn and sugarcane. Cars drove on mud roads, often getting stuck during the rainy months. The setting was a perfect one for a boy who dreamed only of playing baseball.

Hank and his siblings had many chores. They gathered wood to be used to heat the house and cook their food. With so many people to feed, Estella learned how to stretch her supplies. Most of what the Aarons ate came from their garden. The family ate staples like cornbread, greens, and beans. Now and then, they had some pork, beef, or chicken. The kids shared beds and clothing. In fact, Hank thought nothing of wearing his sister's hand-me-downs.

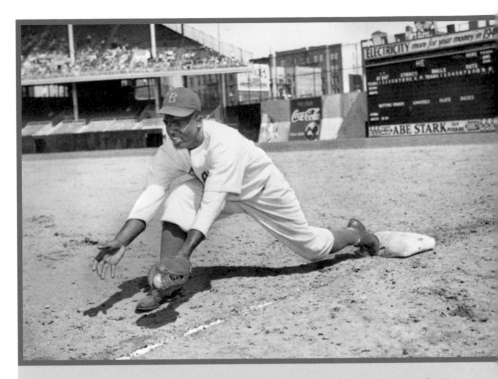

Jackie Robinson fields a ball at first base in April 1947 at Ebbets Field in Brooklyn. Robinson made his debut that season with the Brooklyn Dodgers, becoming the first black player in the major leagues. The following year, Robinson visited Hank Aaron's hometown in Alabama, giving Hank the chance to see his hero and forge his big-league dreams.

Estella worked hard to provide a good home for her husband and her children. Occasionally she took a job cleaning houses, but she spent most of her time keeping the children in line. Herbert worked in the shipyard when he could find work, usually as a boilermaker's assistant. To earn money when he was out of a job, he opened a small tavern next to the family's house. It was called the Black Cat Inn, and it was the only tavern in Toulminville in which black people were allowed to go. People came to drink moonshine, an illegally made alcoholic drink, and dance. Hank's oldest sister, Sarah, ran the tavern. After the neighbors complained about the noise, though, the

Aarons were forced to close the inn. Young Hank mowed lawns and did odd jobs, like picking potatoes or mixing cement, but his heart was not in that kind of work. Even at an early age, baseball was all that was on his mind.

BASEBALL DREAMS

Hank and some of the youngsters in the neighborhood would often get pickup games going in the fields near the pecan groves that bordered his house. When no one was around to play, he practiced hitting a ball with a stick. He learned how to throw a ball onto the roof of his house and hit it when it

☆ ☆ ☆ ☆ ☆

JACKIE ROBINSON

Jackie Robinson was the first black baseball player in the modern era of the major leagues. Born in 1919, Robinson was raised in Pasadena, California. As a youngster, he was an outstanding athlete in several sports. He attended Pasadena Junior College and then the University of California, Los Angeles, where he starred in baseball, football, and track. Robinson led a full life before he played his first game of professional baseball. He enlisted in the U.S. Army in 1942 and attended officer-candidate school. A year later, he was a second lieutenant. After his discharge in 1944, Robinson played professional football for a short time before joining the Kansas City Monarchs of the Negro National League in 1945.

Robinson's stay with the Monarchs was short-lived. Later that year, Branch Rickey, who was president of the Brooklyn Dodgers in the major leagues, signed Robinson to the Dodgers organization. Rickey had been trying to persuade baseball team owners to open their minds to integrated baseball. He thought that Robinson represented great talent, but just as important, he rolled down. Most of the time, he did not have a real baseball. So he made his own by wrapping a piece of hose around a golf ball or by wadding tape into a ball. He even used tin cans and bottle caps. Hank would spend hours in his front yard hitting bottle caps with a piece of broomstick.

Toulminville had plenty of wide-open space, and the neighborhood kids made a baseball diamond in one vacant lot. There, they played until dark. Soon, the village became part of Mobile, and the city built the black residents a rec-reational park that included real baseball diamonds. Hank spent his days after school on those diamonds, playing on

★ ★ ★ ★ ★

saw that Robinson was a man of dignity who would be strong in the face of adversity. Robinson started out with the Montreal Royals, a Dodger minor-league team. He led the league in bat-ting average during his first and only season with the Royals. In 1947, Robinson joined the Dodgers. It was a landmark event that changed baseball forever.

Robinson did not take long to make his mark as a player. He was voted Rookie of the Year and led the league in stolen bases. In 1949, he won the batting title with a .342 average. That year, he was also voted the National League Most Valuable Player. Robinson's success continued until his retirement in 1957. He was inducted into the Baseball Hall of Fame. His autobiography, *I Never Had It Made*, was published in 1972, the year he died. Every major-league team has retired No. 42 to honor Robinson. In 1987, to mark the fortieth anni-versary of Robinson's breaking the color barrier, Major League Baseball renamed the Rookie of the Year award the Jackie Robinson Award.

local teams, usually against teams from Mobile and the surrounding area.

Hank's uncle taught him about baseball, taking the youngster under his wing for a game of catch or some batting practice. Hank, though, was also inspired by more accomplished players, like the legendary Jackie Robinson. In 1947, Robinson became the first black player in the major leagues. He was a hero to Hank and to the other men, women, and children of Toulminville, just as he was to people in other black communities across the country.

One day in 1948, Robinson visited Toulminville, and Hank skipped class to hear him speak. The great player talked at length about baseball and community. Afterward, Hank was inspired to dream bigger dreams, and he thought that one day he, too, might play professional baseball like his hero.

Hank's parents would come to support his dreams, but their backing would not come easily. Herbert and Estella placed a high value on education and insisted that their children's schoolwork come before everything else. Although Hank's father understood his son's need to play baseball, his mother was more reluctant. Her dream was that Hank would attend college and make a better life for himself and for the black community. She even encouraged him to go out for football instead of baseball, because a good athlete like him might earn a football scholarship to college.

Hank, though, wanted nothing to do with football. Baseball was his sport, and he stuck to his guns. He was no prize student, but he at least made a minimal effort at school, if only to appease his mother. Aside from being in the Boy Scouts, Hank spent his early teenage years reading comic books, shooting marbles with friends, and playing ball. It was during this time, in the open fields of Toulminville, that Hank Aaron began to live his dream.

2

A Foot
in the Door

Although Hank Aaron played plenty of baseball in pickup games, neither he nor any other black kids were allowed to play in organized leagues. If African Americans wanted to play organized ball, they played softball in a recreation league. One day when Hank was playing softball, a local man named Ed Scott came to watch, as he sometimes did, with the hope of finding a young prospect for his team. Scott was a player/manager with the Mobile Black Bears, a local semiprofessional baseball team made up of black players, mostly adults.

Right away, Scott saw that Hank had a talent for baseball and wanted him to play for the Black Bears. Hank's mother thought that her son, who was 17, was too young to play on a team of grown men. Furthermore, she wanted him to finish high school and go to college. After a lot of begging from

Hank and Scott, she allowed him to play at the team's home games but not to travel for its away games. So Hank played the Sunday home games in the nearby town of Prichard. As one of the better fielders on the team, he played shortstop. Hank was paid $10 per game, which was a lot of money for him.

Besides managing the Black Bears, Scott was a part-time scout for a more prominent team, the Indianapolis Clowns, which were part of the Negro American League. Scott had been sending reports on the talented young player to the Clowns' management, who grew eager to see Hank in action. Scott arranged for the Clowns to come to Prichard to play the Black Bears so that the Clowns' business manager, Bunny Downs, could get a look at him. Hank hit well that day, and Downs offered him a spot on the team. Hank's mother, though, would have nothing to do with the offer, insisting that Hank return to school in the fall to finish his final year. Downs agreed to send for Hank in the spring when school was out, but Hank figured that Downs would forget all about him.

Hank had bigger dreams. He wanted to play in the major leagues. That summer, the Brooklyn Dodgers held a tryout for black players in Mobile. Hank's idol, Jackie Robinson, played for the Dodgers, as did Roy Campanella, another black player. Hank had a feeling that he would one day play alongside Robinson, so he went to the tryouts with the idea that this was his big chance.

Hank, though, faced stiff competition. Plenty of very good players came to the tryouts, and many were cockier and physically bigger than Hank. It was hard for him to get noticed. When it was his turn to bat, he took only a few swings before a bigger guy pushed him out of the batter's box. Some scouts told him he was too small and would never make the major leagues. Hank was disappointed and no longer as much of a Dodgers fan as he had been. The lesson, though, was a good one for a player who would later face plenty of stinging criticism from racist fans.

Hank went back to school, wondering if the Clowns would come through for him in the spring. That winter, in early 1952, he received a contract in the mail offering him $200 a month to play ball for the Clowns. He was to report to spring training in Winston-Salem, North Carolina. Hank's mother wanted him to finish the year at school, but Hank remembers, "Two hundred dollars was a lot of money to a family like ours." Hank also promised that, if he made the team, he would finish school in the off-season and, if he did not make the team, he would go on to college. His mother allowed him to go, and a few days later, he was on the bus to Winston-Salem.

HANK GETS A BREAK

When Hank arrived in Winston-Salem, he expected to learn about the game and have the chance to showcase his hitting. He found, though, that the other players were not all that interested in him. The Clowns had won the Negro American League championship the previous season, and for the most part, the players thought the team would do just fine with or without his talent. Hank took the veterans' barbs in stride. They poked fun at his ragged clothes, shoes, and glove. They also did not let him bat very often. He mostly watched from the sidelines while the other players practiced.

Hank was learning that ball clubs traditionally give rookies a hard time. It did not help that he was shy and quiet. Most of the players were in their mid-30s and had seen a lot more of the world than Hank had. Unlike his future, their futures were no longer promising. In those days, players stayed in the Negro Leagues and made a couple of hundred dollars a month. Times, though, were changing. These veterans knew that some of the younger players might have a shot at the big leagues, which meant the opportunity for higher salaries and more fame, and they must have held some resentment against a kid like Hank.

The Indianapolis Clowns, pictured in this 1948 photograph, began as a barnstorming team that was known for its slapstick routines. The players were also respected for their baseball skills. In 1952, 18-year-old Hank Aaron received a contract for $200 a month to play for the Clowns, who had won the Negro American League title the year before.

At the time, Hank did not have much hope either. He was getting little practice time. As spring training gave way to exhibition games, though, Hank caught a break. One of the starting infielders became injured, and Hank was put in the lineup. Immediately he began to produce hits. Soon, he settled in and became a consistent player. And around the league, players and managers began to pay attention to him. Syd Pollack, who owned the Clowns, noticed him, too. He wrote a letter to the farm director of the Boston Braves, a major-league team, and mentioned Hank's talents.

At 18 years of age, Hank found himself batting cleanup, the fourth position in the lineup, for the defending Negro American League champions, with his picture on promotional posters that appeared in every town in which the team played. The Clowns traveled through Texas and Oklahoma, then headed through the South and up the East Coast. It was a grueling, often boring, life. The team members got off the bus to play games and then got back on again to head to the next town. They rarely stopped for meals because few restaurants would serve black people. In fact, Hank recalls sitting in a restaurant in Washington after a meal with the team and listening to the cooks in the kitchen break the plates. Their

☆ ☆ ☆ ☆ ☆ ☆
THE BARNSTORMING CLOWNS

Before the Indianapolis Clowns joined the Negro American League, they were a traveling team that emphasized entertainment over competition. They began in 1929 as the Miami Giants and became the Ethiopian Clowns before they settled on Indianapolis as a "home." The Clowns played a brand of baseball that was a combination of slapstick gags and witty miscues. It was a model of entertainment popularized by basketball's Harlem Globetrotters. Some of the stars were Buster Haywood and Goose Tatum (who also played for the Globetrotters).

The Clowns were respected as ballplayers. The crowds, though, came for the comedy. The players pulled stunts like batting in a rocking chair, and the pitchers would often throw the ball behind their backs or through their legs. During the brief warm-ups before the beginning of each inning, they did a "shadowball" routine, in which the players went through the motions of fielding and throwing without the ball.

The Clowns used their comedy to draw white audiences to their games and wowed them with their baseball skills, helping to pave the way for the acceptance of black baseball players.

When the Clowns joined the Negro American League in 1943, the team toned down its antics a bit. After the demise of the Negro Leagues, the Clowns continued as a barnstorming team and returned to their comedy routines. The team remained in operation until the 1980s.

reasoning: No white person would want to eat off those plates even if they had been washed.

The buzz surrounding Hank and his talents had grown into a steady drone, and quite a few major-league teams were interested in the young star. According to Aaron's autobiography, the Chicago *Defender* reported that "major-league scouts are swarming to parks where the Clowns are playing to get a good look at the young Aaron. . . . All seem to agree that he stands at the plate like a Ted Williams."

One day, after Hank had several hits during a game in Buffalo, a man called him over. Dewey Griggs, a scout for the Boston Braves, noticed that Hank grabbed the bat cross-handed, or with the "wrong" hand on top. He introduced himself and told Hank to try to hit with his hands in the correct position—as a right-handed batter, with his right hand on top. Hank gave it a try and hit a home run the first time.

Griggs was impressed and sent a letter to John Mullen, the Braves' farm director, praising Hank's hitting but expressing some concern about his fielding and throwing. Hank tended to throw sidearm to first base and flip the ball underhand to second base. Griggs was looking for a player with a good throwing arm and wanted to see Hank play again. After watching Hank play another game, Griggs was convinced that he had the ability to play in the big leagues. More than a few teams, however, were interested in Hank. In fact, Hank was considered the best prospect in the Negro Leagues since Willie Mays, who at the time was tearing up the majors with his crisp hitting and flashy fielding. Mays's team, the New York Giants, wanted Hank to play alongside Mays.

In late May 1952, as Clowns owner Syd Pollock entertained offers from teams for Hank's services, Hank thought about the pros and cons of playing for each team. On one hand, it would be great to play alongside Mays in New York. On the other, the Braves were willing to pay him a bit more money, and he felt he had a better chance of making that team over the talent-heavy Giants. In the end, the Braves made a better offer, and Hank signed a contract. He would make $350 each month and report to the club's Northern League team in Eau Claire, Wisconsin. This step was an important one for Hank. He had crossed over from the Negro Leagues to the majors and mainstream white culture.

The Minor Leagues

Hank Aaron was not the only one to profit from being picked up by the Boston Braves. Syd Pollock, who owned the rights to Aaron as a player, made several thousand dollars in the deal. He presented the young star with a cardboard suitcase as a signing bonus. On June 8, Aaron played for the Clowns in Chicago, then boarded a small, twin-propeller airplane for the short jaunt to Eau Claire—the first time he had ever flown on a plane.

When Aaron arrived, the team was on the road, so he checked into the local YMCA. The two other African-American players on the team—Julie Bowers and a young player named John "Wes" Covington—were rooming at the Y. Like Aaron, Covington had a promising career ahead of him.

In his autobiography, *I Had a Hammer,* Aaron describes Bowers as a solid player who did not have the talent necessary for the big leagues, "the type of black player you always found on minor-league teams back then—an older guy who was there to provide company for the younger black players and keep them out of trouble." Bowers would show Aaron and Covington the ropes. His expertise was not limited to baseball or how to survive a long road trip. It was specific to the life of a black man in the greater baseball culture, and Aaron would find his advice and guidance invaluable.

PAVING THE WAY

Several previous players on the team had had a major role in paving the way for black players within the Braves organization. Before Aaron, a few other black players were on the team in Eau Claire—some of them very well received. One was Bill Bruton, who was the Northern League Rookie of the Year two years before Aaron joined the team. Bruton was an exciting player to watch, and he was respected off the field as well. He became the most popular member of the team during his season at Eau Claire. Another player was Horace Garner, an outfielder with exceptional skills. He also was named the league's Rookie of the Year, the year after Bruton won the award.

These players did some of the hard work in introducing the white team members and the city to black baseball players. The team and the city more readily accepted Aaron, even though he was quiet. He still felt, however, that people were paying closer attention to him—"looking at me as though I were some kind of strange creature," as he wrote in his autobiography. It was not easy. He and the other black ballplayers were essentially the only people who were not white in Eau Claire. Aaron handled the pressure well. His attitude was that the skeptics were simply ignorant and had had little interaction with black people. He was there to prove them wrong.

What was different, and in some ways scary, for Aaron was playing against white players. All his life, he had suited up on

☆ ☆ ☆ ☆ ☆ ☆

THE NEGRO LEAGUES

African Americans began to play "organized" baseball in the mid-1800s. In the 1860s, a handful of amateur teams were fairly well known in the black communities in which they played. All-black professional teams started to play in the 1880s. These teams included the St. Louis Black Stockings and the Cuban Giants (of New York).

In 1884, two African Americans played briefly in the major leagues. Moses Fleetwood Walker joined the Toledo Blue Stockings in 1883, and the following year, the team joined the American Association, one of two major leagues at the time. Walker played in 42 games that season, hitting .263, while his brother, Welday Walker, played in six games for Toledo. The Toledo team folded after 1884, and Moses Walker returned to the minor leagues.

During the 1890s and the early twentieth century, most professional all-black teams traveled parts of the country to play in exhibition games on the barnstorming circuit. Some major-league players joined the barnstorming teams when the regular season was over.

On February 13, 1920, in a YMCA in Kansas City, Missouri, Andrew "Rube" Foster, owner of the Chicago American Giants, founded the first successful Negro League. Foster served as president of the league and was called "the father of black baseball." The first season of the Negro National League featured the Chicago American Giants, the Chicago Giants, the Cuban all-black teams in all-black leagues. All his life, he had been told that black people were inferior to white people, and for the first time in his life, he would have the chance to compare his game with that of white ballplayers. "I never doubted my ability," he

★ ★ ★ ★ ★ ★

Stars, the Dayton Marcos, the Indianapolis ABCs, the Kansas City Monarchs, and the St. Louis Giants. In 1929, the Great Depression hit the United States, causing widespread financial hardship. As a result, fewer fans were able to afford tickets to games. Foster's league did not survive. Following the 1931 season, the original Negro National League disbanded after 11 years in existence.

In 1933, a new Negro National League emerged—established by Gus Greenlee, who owned the Pittsburgh Crawfords. Four years later, the Negro American League was formed, with teams in the Midwest and the South. The Negro National League and the Negro American League were the premier leagues. There were other leagues as well, including the Negro Southern League and the Texas Negro League.

Most people considered Negro League players to be of the same caliber as the white players in the major leagues. Times were changing, though, with Jackie Robinson, a former Negro League player, reaching the majors in 1947. By the end of the 1952 season, more than 150 former Negro League players were suiting up in the major and minor leagues. Robinson's triumphant move to the major leagues was the beginning of the end of the Negro Leagues. As major-league teams snatched up the best African-American players, the quality of play in the Negro Leagues suffered. As a result, fewer fans attended games, and the great era of Negro League baseball came to a close.

Hank Aaron *(right)* is shown with fellow Milwaukee Braves outfielders John "Wes" Covington *(left)* and Bill Bruton during spring training in 1958 in Bradenton, Florida. All three shared a history on the Eau Claire, Wisconsin, minor-league team. Covington and Aaron were teammates there in 1952—two of only three black players on the team. Aaron was named the league's Rookie of the Year. Bruton played in Eau Claire two years earlier and also was Rookie of the Year.

wrote in *I Had a Hammer*, "but when you hear all your life that you're inferior, it makes you wonder if the other guys have something you've never seen before."

With his first at-bat, Aaron quickly proved that he could hit, regardless of the color of the pitcher's skin. He smacked a single. His second time up, he singled again. Because of his strong start, Aaron was immediately moved up in the batting order from seventh to second.

MAKING HIS MARK

It was not all rosy, though, for the young man. It was lonely being away from home and in a "white" world. Nothing was as Aaron was used to. People behaved differently from those in his community in Alabama. The customs were different. The food was different. He did not really feel as if he could be himself on or off the field. He considered packing up his cardboard suitcase and leaving Eau Claire for his home in Mobile. He called his parents and told one of his brothers that he was coming home. His brother told him that, if he left, he would be "walking out on the best break" he would ever see. Aaron realized that his brother was right and that, if he quit, he would never get the chance to see how he measured up against the best players in the country. For Aaron, having doubts about his place in the world of white baseball and then speaking to his brother was like taking one last look at his past. It was a moment of truth for the young slugger. From then on, Aaron never looked back.

Aaron soon made his mark in Eau Claire. In mid-June, just a few weeks after he started to play for the team, he was leading the league in hitting. By mid-July, he was asked to play in the Northern League All-Star Game. He hit a single in the game but later sprained his ankle sliding into second. Aaron was doing well, and so was his team. Eau Claire went on a 10-game winning streak before eventually finishing third in the league. Aaron batted .336, second-highest in the league. The big news was that he was named the league's Rookie of the Year.

After the season ended, Aaron returned to the Indianapolis Clowns and found himself playing in the Negro American League's World Series. The series traveled to several cities, including Mobile. The trip was the first time Aaron had returned to Mobile since he left on the bus for spring training. Aaron began to see the impact he was having on his hometown. The day of the first game in Mobile was named Hank Aaron Day. Everyone came out to see him, and he was overwhelmed.

To top it off, the Clowns went on to win the series. Afterward, Aaron returned to Mobile for the winter. His mother insisted that he return to high school and earn his diploma. Aaron found that even a minor-league Rookie of the Year had to heed his mother's advice. "I knew there was no getting around it," Aaron wrote in his autobiography. "No matter what I did on the ball field, Mama wasn't going to cut me loose until I graduated from high school."

4

Class A

Many people believe that, after Jackie Robinson played his first major-league game, all of baseball became desegregated. In reality, though, only baseball in the Northern United States became desegregated. The Dodgers played most of their games in Northern states, where the laws and customs were more tolerant of racial integration. The major leagues had no teams farther south than St. Louis. Once, Robinson had been forbidden to play in an exhibition game with the Brooklyn Dodgers in Jacksonville, Florida. When the Dodgers defied local law enforcement officials and arrived at the stadium with Robinson, the players found the gates padlocked. Jacksonville would have rather canceled a baseball game than seen one played with a black man on the field. For Hank Aaron, his next minor-league stint would take him here, to the South, where integration was a harder pill to swallow.

TAKING THE FIELD IN THE DEEP SOUTH

During spring training in 1953, the Boston Braves moved to Milwaukee, Wisconsin. The new Milwaukee Braves sent two African Americans—Aaron and Horace Garner—and a player from Puerto Rico, Felix Mantilla, to its farm team in Jacksonville, the city that had barred Robinson from playing just six years earlier. Jacksonville was part of the South Atlantic League, otherwise known as the Sally League. The league was at a higher level in baseball's farm system than the Northern League. So the players were more competitive than those Aaron had played with and against a season earlier. For Aaron, the move was a big step up, but he would also be subjected to more racial discrimination in Jacksonville than in Eau Claire. Aaron, Garner, and Mantilla would have to be the players to break the color barrier in Jacksonville, and that would not be easy.

When Aaron was sent to Jacksonville, he was told he was being moved from shortstop to second base because Mantilla was more proficient at shortstop. Aaron was confident that he was ready to play at this level. He knew that the Braves' management had the belief that he and the other black players on the team could pave the way for black players in the future, just as Billy Bruton had done for him in Eau Claire.

Their presence brought black spectators to the games. Wherever the team played, attendance records were set because black fans—a new group of fans—were coming to see them play. Still, not everyone was happy to see these players on the field. Aaron had to endure racial slurs from the white fans without being able to respond, and he still had to concentrate on the game. Frequently, white pitchers tried to hit him with the ball. That did not anger Aaron so

Hank Aaron, then in the Braves' minor-league system, poses for a portrait during spring training in 1953. That year, he was sent to play for the Braves' farm team in Jacksonville, Florida, in the South Atlantic League. Six years earlier, the city of Jacksonville had barred Jackie Robinson from playing an exhibition game there.

much as puzzle him. It was important that Aaron and the other black players not lose their heads or it would be harder for black players to follow them. All eyes were on them.

☆ ☆ ☆ ☆ ☆ ☆

SATCHEL PAIGE

Leroy Robert "Satchel" Paige was one of the most feared pitchers in baseball. He pitched in the Negro Leagues and the major leagues, on barnstorming teams, and for teams in Cuba and the Dominican Republic. The charismatic Paige was one reason that major-league teams started to look at black players.

Paige was born in Mobile, Alabama, not far from where Hank Aaron would be born some years later. Paige's date of birth is thought to be July 7, 1906, but no one knows for sure. Paige was the seventh of 12 children. As a boy, he was frequently in trouble. He helped carry passengers' luggage at the train station for small change and was given the nickname "Satchel" because he once tried to steal a bag. Eventually, he was sent to a juvenile detention school after being caught shoplifting. At the school, he learned how to pitch.

Paige began to pitch professionally in 1926 with the Chattanooga Black Lookouts of the Negro Southern League. He got off to a rocky start, but then a teammate taught him the "hesitation pitch," which he used to great effect. Paige soon left the Lookouts for a team in the highly regarded Negro National League, setting a pattern of short stays with ball clubs that would characterize his career. In 1929, he set a record for strikeouts in a single season with 184. Paige became such a draw that his team's owner rented him out to other teams now and then to draw bigger crowds.

Paige bounced around more than 10 Negro League teams, earning a reputation as the best pitcher in the United States.

Jacksonville played against teams in places like Savannah and Augusta, Georgia; Montgomery, Alabama; and Columbia, South Carolina. Aaron, Garner, and Mantilla braced themselves

☆ ☆ ☆ ☆ ☆

His personality was legendary, too. In one game early in his career, he called in his outfielders to sit in the infield while he completed the inning. He often struck out 10 to 15 players a game. Along the way, he became the highest-paid athlete in the world, earning more than even the white stars in the major leagues.

In the mid-1940s, Branch Rickey, one of the architects of integration in Major League Baseball, was looking for a player from the Negro Leagues to make the jump. Everyone thought that player would be Paige. Rickey instead chose Jackie Robinson, a younger, more even-tempered player. Paige eventually made it to the majors midway through the 1948 season, when he joined the Cleveland Indians. At 42, he was baseball's oldest rookie. Throughout his career, Paige continued to barnstorm, more often than not playing for whichever team would pay him the most.

His last full season in the majors was 1953. After several years in and out of baseball, Paige signed to pitch for the Portland Beavers, a minor-league team, in 1962. He was 56 years old. The Kansas City A's of the major leagues signed him for one game at age 59. Paige pitched off and on until 1967, when he finally hung up his cleats. Throughout his career, Paige is credited with more than 300 shutouts in 1,500 wins. In 1971, he became the first player from the Negro Leagues to be inducted into the Baseball Hall of Fame. Paige died on June 8, 1982.

for the slurs, and with good reason. They heard all kinds of cruel rants and even had bottles and rocks thrown at them while they were on the field. In more than one instance, the FBI was called in when death threats were made. Many times when they left a ballpark, one of them carried a baseball bat as an extra measure of protection. Even some of their white teammates did not accept them. Aaron, Garner, and Mantilla stayed in separate hotels and did not eat with the white players.

Yet none of this hurt Aaron's game. By mid-season, he was one of the Sally League's leading hitters and was chosen for the league's All-Star Game. Even better, the team was doing well, having already eliminated most of its competitors from the pennant race. Aaron was developing the confidence that finally led him to believe that he might have a secure future in baseball.

MAKING A DIFFERENCE

Despite experiencing racism from a majority of white fans, Aaron and his teammates were treated well by others. Local merchants would give out gifts as incentives to players who did well. Aaron received watches and clothes, among other items, and he soon acquired a wardrobe worthy of the other guys on the squad. A look at his batting stats would show why. That year, he led the league with a .362 batting average and 125 RBIs.

Aaron, however, also led the league in errors, with 36. Compared with other players, he had been a bad shortstop, and he was an even worse second baseman. Despite his overall athletic ability, Aaron lacked the quick footwork required of major-league infielders, and he looked uncomfortable at shortstop and at second base. Fortunately, the team's coaches recognized that his speed and his strong arm would be assets to their outfield. They agreed they should try him in the outfield. Immediately, Aaron felt at home at his new position in right field.

Shortstop Felix Mantilla was a teammate of Hank Aaron's on the Braves as well as on the Jacksonville farm team in 1953. Aaron, Mantilla, and Horace Garner—the only players of color on the Jacksonville team—endured racial slurs from white spectators and had bottles and rocks thrown at them. Still, the season was gratifying for Aaron. In his autobiography, he wrote: "We had shown them that the South wouldn't fall off the map if we played in their ballparks."

The team made the playoffs, with much celebration. Even though Jacksonville lost the best-of-seven series to Columbia, the year was an important one for the team and for the entire Braves organization. Jacksonville had proven that it had the talent to play with the best in the league. The Braves had a bright future, and Aaron was right in the middle of it.

In *I Had a Hammer*, Aaron wrote:

> We were disappointed to lose the playoffs, but Horace [Garner] and Felix [Mantilla] and I didn't lose sight of what we accomplished that summer. We had played a season of great baseball in the Deep South, under circumstances that nobody had experienced before and—because of us—never would again. We had shown the people of Georgia and Alabama and South Carolina and Florida that we were good ballplayers and decent human beings, and that all it took to get along together was to get a little more used to each other. We had shown them that the South wouldn't fall off the map if we played in their ballparks.

Aaron called it the most gratifying part of the summer and the most important thing he has ever done in his life. "It showed that things were changing a little, and we were part of the reason why."

That year, Aaron was named the league's most valuable player. The night of the awards banquet, he called Barbara Lucas, a woman from Jacksonville he had been dating for some time, and proposed marriage. The two were married on October 6, 1953, and stayed with Aaron's parents for a while. Then, Mantilla invited Hank and Barbara to travel with him to Puerto Rico for winter baseball, which American major-league ballplayers often did. Aaron would have a great opportunity to see how he could hit against major-league pitchers. As it turned out, it was also a great chance for him to see how he fared in the outfield. Aaron played so well against the major-league pitchers in the winter league that he made the all-star team. It was his third all-star team in three leagues within a two-year span.

Breakthrough to the Big Leagues

As Hank Aaron and his teammates were suffering racism in Jacksonville and the other cities in the Sally League, issues surrounding race relations were coming to a boil across the country. The civil rights movement, the force of people who rallied against segregation and would be integral to changing segregationist laws, was about to be born. In 1954, which was Hank Aaron's rookie year in the big leagues, a landmark event took place that helped to bring the issues surrounding racism and the treatment of African Americans to the forefront of the collective American mind. Oliver Brown, a black man from Topeka, Kansas, had petitioned to allow his daughter to go to a nearby white school rather than to the black school, which was farther away. The Brown case was combined with four similar cases from across the country, and as *Brown v. the Board of Education of Topeka,* the case made its way to the United States Supreme Court. On May 17, 1954, the Supreme Court unanimously ruled that "separate educational facilities are inherently unequal."

THE GREAT EXPERIMENT

When the *Brown v. the Board of Education* ruling was made, desegregation had already begun in baseball. In 1945, Branch Rickey, the president and general manager of the Brooklyn Dodgers, lobbied baseball to allow Jackie Robinson to play on the Dodgers' farm team in Montreal. The owners of the 15 other major-league teams were against the proposal. The commissioner of baseball, Albert "Happy" Chandler, however, overruled the owners and allowed the team to sign Robinson.

When Robinson came up to the majors in 1947, he experienced verbal abuse from all corners—fans, opponents, teammates, the front office, the press. In fact, a group of white players around the league signed a petition saying they would never play on the same field as a black player. Players spit on him. Pitchers threw beanballs, pitches aimed to hit a batter in the head. Baseball had made an example of Robinson, and racist America did its best to return the favor.

One reason that Rickey selected Robinson for this groundbreaking role was his character. He was unflappable, and he showed unimaginable restraint in holding his tongue against an onslaught of racial slurs and prejudice. Rickey knew that, if Robinson could keep his cool, the furor over black players in baseball would simmer down. As it turned out, Robinson did keep his head. He withstood a variety of attacks and never lost his composure in public.

Following Robinson were Willie Mays, Roy Campanella, Don Newcombe and another dozen black players. All were subject to the same treatment that Robinson received. The tide, though, was beginning to turn by the time Aaron was poised to break into the majors. It would not be long before black players were on the rosters of every major-league team. (The Boston Red Sox were the last team to integrate, signing Pumpsie Green in 1959.)

☆ ☆ ☆ ☆ ☆ ☆

RACIAL SEGREGATION IN THE UNITED STATES

Racial segregation is the separation of people of different races. Segregation was mandated by state and local laws that required the separation of whites and blacks in all public places. These laws, known as "Jim Crow" laws, were in force from 1876 to 1964, mainly in Southern states. Jim Crow laws were primarily enforced in public buildings and in schools. By extension, whites embraced segregation as the norm on public transportation and in restaurants and parks. African Americans used separate restrooms and drinking fountains and bought their ice cream from "colored-only" windows at ice cream parlors. Segregation existed as a rule in the armed forces. Jim Crow laws also affected voting, as Southern states instituted literacy tests and poll taxes in an effort to deny the vote to black people.

Pressure to end segregation grew strong in the late 1940s. *Brown v. Board of Education of Topeka* (1954) was a landmark case that overturned the legality of segregation in public schools. Several incidents caught the nation's attention and helped to create political pressure to expand the scope of *Brown*. One incident occurred on a city bus in December 1955 in Montgomery, Alabama, when Rosa Parks refused to give up her seat to a white man, as was the custom. Her arrest led to

A DREAM COME TRUE

In 1954, Hank Aaron came to spring training wondering if he would make the Milwaukee Braves or return to the minor leagues. He knew the team had solid players in center field and right field, and during the off-season, the Braves traded for left fielder Bobby Thomson of the New York Giants. Aaron

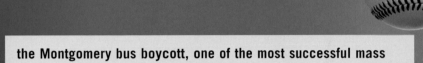

the Montgomery bus boycott, one of the most successful mass movements against segregation.

The organizers of the boycott, who included the Reverend Martin Luther King, Jr., joined with other church leaders and activists to form the Southern Christian Leadership Conference in 1957. The organization, which was based in Atlanta, supported local efforts to fight segregation.

In August 1963, Dr. King led the March on Washington, which brought civil-rights concerns into the living rooms of the United States. The march drew more than 200,000 demonstrators to the Lincoln Memorial in Washington, D.C. There, Dr. King made his famous "I Have a Dream" speech: "I have a dream," he said, "that one day this nation will rise up and live out the true meaning of its creed: We hold these truths to be self-evident, that all men are created equal."

The march helped to propel passage of the Civil Rights Act of 1964, which outlawed discrimination based on race, color, religion, sex, or national origin in the areas of voting, employment, and public services, like transportation and schools. Soon after, Congress passed the Voting Rights Act of 1965, which outlawed the requirement that potential voters pass literacy tests to register to vote.

A police officer fingerprints Rosa Parks in Montgomery, Alabama, after she was charged with violating racial segregation laws. In December 1955, Parks refused to give up her seat on a city bus to a white man. Her action helped to start the Montgomery bus boycott, a 13-month boycott of the public transit system.

did not even think he was in line to be the first backup in the outfield. Aaron, though, was about to get the chance of a lifetime. When Thomson broke his ankle in spring training, Aaron found himself with the opportunity to make the starting lineup. He took advantage of this chance in a spring-training game against the Red Sox in Sarasota, Florida, when he hit an impressively long home run. He was given a major-league contract and the starting job on the spot.

When the Braves and the Brooklyn Dodgers played against each other in the preseason, Aaron was able to fulfill his boyhood dream: to play on the same field as Jackie Robinson. The Braves and the Dodgers traveled together, playing exhibition games as the teams made their way north for the regular season. Aaron and Robinson played in a game together in front of Aaron's family in Mobile. Aaron hit a single and a double that day and was quite proud. During this barnstorming trip, Aaron spent quite a bit of time off the field shadowing Robinson and the other black players, who counseled him on what to expect in the majors and how to deal with the racism he would surely encounter.

Aaron notes in *I Had a Hammer* that he realized that, no matter how he tried to fit in, he would never be just another player: He was a black player, and he would be treated differently by everyone who was part of the game. Some players would hate him no matter how good he was. He believed he had to be good. In *Hank Aaron, the Home Run That Changed America*, he said, "Black people had been crying out for opportunity in this country for two centuries, and finally we had it. Our mission—and that's the only thing to call it—was to do something with the chance we had."

Aaron, though, still had to hit the ball. Early in the season, he found that hard to do. Aaron went hitless in his first game in the majors on April 13 and did not get a hit until two days later—a double against the St. Louis Cardinals. A week later, Aaron hit his first major-league home run. From then on, he felt much better about his chances as a player.

At the time, Willie Mays, the flamboyant New York Giants outfielder, was taking the National League by storm. He led the league in hitting and was a flashy outfielder. He was widely marketed as the "Say Hey Kid." Merchandise featuring Mays included comic books and special caps. Even songs were written about him. Mays was the player with whom Aaron was most often compared throughout his career. But back in 1954, a far as the Braves were concerned, Aaron was just filling in for the injured Bobby Thomson.

Hank Aaron made it to the major leagues in 1954. Here, he is pictured at the Polo Grounds in New York during the exhibition season that year. Aaron had his first chance to play in a game against his idol, Jackie Robinson. Robinson and other black players also served as mentors to Aaron, telling him what to expect in the major leagues.

In his first year, Aaron hit .280, a respectable average but below what he was used to hitting. In September, near the end of the season, he broke his ankle while sliding into third base. Thomson, by now healthy, was sent in as a pinch runner for Aaron and took Aaron's place for the remaining games. Aaron's season was over.

"By the end of the season, I knew I belonged in the big leagues, but I was a little disappointed in myself. It was probably because I figured I ought to lead any league I played in," Aaron wrote in his autobiography. He would, soon enough.

6

Rising Star

In 1955, Hank Aaron's second year in the big leagues, he was beginning to adjust to the lifestyle of a ballplayer and to the level of play on the field. Though players in the majors were treated better than those in the minors, riding trains instead of buses on road trips for instance, he was still subject to the racism that was part of the culture.

On the field, he was becoming familiar with some of the pitchers he had faced the previous year. His batting average went up, and he began to get a reputation as a player who could crush the ball. A journalist gave him the nickname "Hammerin' Hank," which stayed with him throughout his career. Aaron played in his first All-Star Game in 1955. In it, he sat on the bench until late in the game, when he drove in the tying run, sending the game into extra innings.

Hank Aaron is pictured with Wally Moon *(left)* and Stan Musial, both of the St. Louis Cardinals, before a game in August 1956 in St. Louis. Aaron was leading the league in batting, Moon was second, and Musial was third. Aaron would go on to win the National League batting title that year, with a .328 average.

That year, Aaron hit .314 with 27 home runs, far short of the 51 home runs that Willie Mays put on the board. But Aaron was improving, and so were the Braves. They finished second in the National League that season. Aaron was named the Braves'

Most Valuable Player and was given a salary of $17,000 for the next year. After the season, he played with Willie Mays's barnstorming team, which was made up of some of the better black players from the major leagues as well as some stars from the Negro Leagues. They traveled by car, playing games and splitting the money that was earned.

Aaron had a breakout season in 1956 and helped lead the team into the thick of the race to win the National League pennant. For Aaron, this was baseball at its best. At midseason, the Braves took over first place, but they were in a tough battle with the Brooklyn Dodgers and the Cincinnati Reds. The season ended with Brooklyn winning the pennant, a game ahead of the Braves and two ahead of the Reds. Aaron hit .328 to lead the National League in hitting. He also led the league in hits with 200 and total bases with 340. At one point during the season, he went on a 25-game hitting streak. *Sporting News* named him the National League Player of the Year. The batting title and the other awards that came his way were huge honors for such a young player, and particularly for a black player. Still, Aaron and the Braves were crushed that they did not win the pennant and play in the World Series.

RACE TO THE PENNANT

In 1957, Aaron had settled into a comfortable zone with big-league pitching. Life was good in Milwaukee, and the Braves felt they had a certain chemistry that would push them to success. This feeling was shared by the fans. It was clear that after only four years, Milwaukee loved its Braves.

After losing the pennant in '56, Braves manager Fred Haney wanted to make sure the team would be ready for anything. Spring training saw the players doing boot-camp-style physical exercises to whip them into shape. Aaron responded well to praise, and Haney would occasionally speak well about the young player to some of the reporters who covered the team. He said that Aaron would be one of the greatest hitters in the game. Such compliments motivated Aaron. The batting title he won the year before also motivated him.

Aaron wanted to win another significant and important honor, so he set a target of winning the Triple Crown, which goes to a player who leads the league in home runs, runs batted in, and batting average—a difficult and rare feat. Ted Williams of the Boston Red Sox was one of only two players in the history of baseball to achieve the Triple Crown twice—in 1942 and 1947 in the American League. Rogers Hornsby won it twice in the National League, in 1922 and 1925. The Yankees' Mickey Mantle was the latest winner, taking the American League Triple Crown in 1956. Aaron thought he could achieve it if he just kept hitting the way he always had. That is, he used his strong, quick wrists to smack the ball all over the field, even to right field, or "the opposite field."

Aaron got off to a hot start that season. He hit a home run in the opening game against the Reds. Later, he had five singles in one game, then drove in four runs the following day. He was hitting like mad. Then he went on a home-run streak, hitting seven in eight days. Suddenly, players and reporters began to think of him as a home-run hitter. Aaron later said he was not consciously focusing on hitting home runs. He added, though, that he might have subconsciously been affected by the publicity and the big money that home-run hitters like Eddie Mathews, a Braves teammate, and Willie Mays received. Many of his teammates agreed. They had seen Aaron be competitive with Mathews, who was also his friend, and thought that the competition motivated him. Whatever his motivation, Aaron was red-hot. And not only was he hitting home runs, he was hitting for average, too. Aaron was right up there with the league leaders in all categories. It looked as if he just might win the coveted Triple Crown.

As Aaron got hot, so did the Braves. Their one weakness, though, was at second base. They needed to fill that gap in the lineup if they were to contend for the pennant. Just past the midway point of the season, the team traded several players to the New York Giants for infielder Red Schoendienst, a veteran and a superb defensive player. Now there was no excuse for losing. In mid-season, the Braves fell into second place amid a five-team pennant race. Aaron suffered a sprained ankle that took him out of the lineup. His recovery was supposed to take two weeks. After only a few days, though, Braves center fielder Bill Bruton, one of Aaron's best friends on the team, suffered a serious injury to his knee. With Bruton out, Aaron felt the pressure to return to the field to help the Braves in the pennant race. So he took Bruton's place in center field, a position he had never played before.

As soon as he returned to the lineup, Aaron was hitting the ball well. In his first game back, the Braves and the Dodgers were tied in the ninth when Aaron came to bat. He scorched a two-run homer to win the game. The next day, he hit a three-run homer and beat the Dodgers with a two-run double. The team regained first place, then traded the lead with several teams until early August. During this magical month, everything fell into place for the Braves. At one point, they won 10 games in a row. The second-place St. Louis Cardinals spun into a nosedive, losing nine consecutive games. With two-thirds of the season played, the Braves had a comfortable lead in the league.

The Cardinals were not finished. They returned to their winning ways, and the Braves cooled off. There was plenty of fear around the Braves clubhouse that the team was about to repeat its performance of '56, when it lost a big lead and the pennant. The mood grew worse when the Cardinals swept the Braves in a doubleheader at the start of September and gained valuable ground. The Cardinals got as close as two games behind the Braves before the Braves opened the gap to four games. The season was winding down. By the third week in September, the Braves led by five games when the Cardinals came to County Stadium for a season-ending showdown. It was their last chance to steal the pennant from the Braves. Based on the Braves' performance the year before, the players and fans were probably nervous about the last few games.

LEAGUE CHAMPIONS

The first game of the series was sold out, and thousands more fans crowded around television sets and radios tuned into the broadcast. The Braves needed to win only one game to take the pennant, but they had not had much luck in their last several games against the Cardinals. On a chilly night, the two teams played the first game of the series. It was so cold that the Cardinals' pitchers built a fire in the bullpen.

The Braves had plenty of chances to score, but they could not move their base runners. The game was tied, 2-2, in extra innings when Aaron came up to bat against a pitcher named William Muffet. Muffet's wicked breaking ball terrified hitters, who rarely made solid contact. In fact, Muffet had not given up a home run all season. A man was on first; a hit might advance the runner or even drive him home. The pressure was on Aaron.

Aaron knew Muffet. He had faced him several times before, and he knew Muffet's best pitch was a curveball. So he waited for a curveball. Aaron's strategy was usually to guess which pitch a pitcher would throw in a given situation. He knew that, if he got ahead in the count, a pitcher was more likely to throw his best pitch to try to get him out. Sure enough, Muffet threw a curveball, and Aaron blasted it into the outfield.

All eyes were on the ball as it sailed long and far toward the center-field wall. The center fielder drifted back to the wall and, as the ball came down, he raised his glove and leaped up to catch the ball. As he stretched to make the catch, the ball sailed just over his glove, over the fence, and into the grass. Aaron had hit a home run, driving in the winning runs and capturing the pennant for the Braves.

The crowd cheered wildly. Aaron's teammates picked him up and carried him off the field. The Braves had won the pennant! Aaron had always dreamed of making a special play for his team, of having a defining moment. This was his, at least for the time being.

The night after the Braves clinched the pennant, they played the Cardinals again. Aaron's heroics continued. When he came up to the plate, he heard the delirious cheers of fans who continued to reward him for hitting the home run that won the pennant. The bases were loaded, and he delivered a grand slam. For the Cardinals, it was salt in the wound.

For Aaron, though, this homer had a greater significance. It was his forty-fourth home run, one more than Ernie Banks had

★ ★ ★ ★ ☆

IN HIS OWN WORDS

"Guessing what the pitcher is going to throw is 80 percent of being a successful hitter. The other 20 percent is just execution. The mental aspects of hitting were especially important to me. I was strictly a guess hitter, which meant I had to have a full knowledge of every pitcher I came up against and develop a strategy for hitting him. My method was to identify the pitches a certain pitcher had and eliminate all but one or two and then wait for them. One advantage I had was quick wrists. Another advantage I had—and one that all good hitters have—was my eyesight. Sometimes I could read the pitcher's grip on the ball before he ever released it and be able to tell what pitch he was throwing. I never worried about the fastball. They couldn't throw it past me, none of them."

—Hank Aaron, from *I Had a Hammer*

Hank Aaron's Milwaukee Braves teammates carry him off the field after the team won the National League pennant in 1957. Aaron's home run in the eleventh inning of a game against the St. Louis Cardinals gave the Braves the win and the pennant.

and enough for Aaron to win his first home-run title. Aaron also won the RBI crown that year, with 132 runs batted in. He fell short, though, of the Triple Crown. At .322, his batting average was good enough for third in the league but was well below that of league leader Stan Musial's .351.

THE 1957 WORLD SERIES

That year, baseball's most celebrated team, the New York Yankees, won the American League pennant and would meet the Braves in the World Series. It was the big-market Bronx Bombers against the small-town Braves. It was David versus Goliath.

Those pairings, though, were not enough for the sportswriters. They needed a more basic element, a one-on-one matchup that would illustrate the human struggle. Taking the best players from each team, they pitted Aaron against Yankee standout Mickey Mantle. Mantle was considered the best player in the game. He was also a fan favorite. Everyone hoped it would be a series to remember.

Aaron had butterflies before the first game. After all, this was the World Series, the grand stage of baseball. The first two games were played at Yankee Stadium in New York. The Yankees won the first game, but the Braves won the second. The series moved to Milwaukee's County Stadium. In the third game, Mantle was injured when a Braves infielder fell on him while reaching for an errant throw from the pitcher. Mantle hurt his shoulder and could not play up to his potential. After all the hype about Mantle vs. Aaron, Mantle would not be a factor in the series. Still, the Yankees won the third game—which was the first World Series game ever played in Milwaukee.

The Yankees led the series two games to one. The pressure was on the Braves. If they lost the fourth game, the Yankees would need to win only one more game to clinch the World Series. Game 4 included one of the most famous moments in baseball. Aaron had hit a three-run homer in the fourth inning to put the Braves up, 4-1.

The lead did not last. The Yankees' Elston Howard hit a clutch home run in the ninth inning to tie the game. In the next inning, Tony Kubek singled, and Hank Bauer hit a triple to drive in the run and give the Yankees the lead. The Braves needed a run in the bottom of the tenth inning to tie the game, or they would be down three games to one in the series, a deficit that would be hard to overcome.

When first baseman Nippy Jones came to the plate, there was little expectation that he would be the one to change the game. Jones was a journeyman who had been in and out of

Hank Aaron slugs a home run in Game 4 of the 1957 World Series against the New York Yankees at County Stadium in Milwaukee. Aaron ended up hitting three home runs in the World Series. He was also named the National League's Most Valuable Player for the 1957 season.

the major leagues for much of his career. When Yankee pitcher Tommy Byrne threw a low pitch, umpire Augie Donatelli called a ball. Jones, though, argued with Donatelli that the pitch had hit his foot.

The two went at it for some time until Jones grabbed the ball from the ground and showed Donatelli the scuff of black shoe polish that had rubbed off onto the ball. Donatelli granted Jones first base, and the Braves had a base runner. The next batter drove Jones home to tie the game. Then up came Braves star Eddie Mathews, who drove the ball into the stands for a game-winning homer. The World Series was tied at two games apiece. The Braves were back in it.

The Braves won Game 5 in a 1-0 pitchers' duel. Game 6 was played in New York. Aaron homered to tie the game at 2-2, but the Yankees scored in the bottom of the seventh inning and went on to win the game. Again the series was tied, with only one game remaining. The team that won Game 7 would win the World Series. That team would be the Braves, as they shut out the Yankees, 5-0, to stun the favored Bronx Bombers.

Aaron performed well in the series, batting .393 with three home runs. It was the World Series ring, though, that mattered most to the slugger. Later he was named the National League's Most Valuable Player. "I was thrilled to be selected and proud to be recognized," he recounted in *I Had a Hammer*. He called 1957 the best year of his baseball life. He was only 23 years old.

The Greatness of Hank Aaron

It seemed that Hank Aaron was on top of the world. His accomplishments were celebrated in Mobile in the off-season, when he was given the key to the city during a special "Hank Aaron Day." He was a World Series hero, widely recognized as one of the best players in the league. Life was going well with Barbara. Still, something gnawed at him. It was racism, and he continued to see it every day.

Aaron had always been reserved about expressing his opinions on race relations to anyone but his family and close friends. Inside of him, though, the seeds of activism were beginning to germinate. He realized that, as a hero, he had influence. The normally reserved man began to speak out to reporters. He limited the focus of his comments to baseball, in which he had credibility. He began to push for change when he talked about segregation in spring training—black and white players still had separate living quarters—and the lack of black managers in the game.

Though he made these comments, much of the media were not interested in painting a World Series hero as an outspoken activist, particularly if he was black. Black-interest magazines like *Jet* and *Ebony*, however, printed his remarks, and he quietly began to develop a reputation as more than just a shy, humble ballplayer.

DEFENDING THE CHAMPIONSHIP

In 1958, the world-champion Braves had high expectations. They rolled through the regular season and clinched the pennant with little drama. Again, they met the Yankees in the World Series. The Braves took a three-games-to-one lead, but the Yanks won Game 5 to send the series back to Milwaukee. The confident Braves did not believe they could lose two straight in Milwaukee, but the Yankees proved them wrong. They won both of the remaining games and were the new world champions. Although the Braves had a solid and talented team, they lacked the magic that had carried them through the 1957 World Series. Aaron had nine hits in the series. During the regular season, he batted .326 and won his first Gold Glove award, signifying his outstanding defensive play.

In 1959, Aaron continued to tear up the league with his hitting. He batted well over .400 during the first half of the season and had a 22-game hitting streak at one point. He was voted again to the National League All-Star team—the first player ever unanimously elected. (Back then, managers, coaches, and players selected the All-Star team.) In that game, he drove in the tying run and scored the winning run on Willie Mays's triple.

That year, three teams were battling for the pennant: the Braves, the Los Angeles Dodgers, and the San Francisco Giants.

Hank Aaron bowls over New York Yankee first baseman Bill Skowron to beat out an infield hit in Game 6 of the 1958 World Series. The Milwaukee Braves held a three-games-to-one lead over the Yankees in the series, but the Yankees captured the next three games to defeat the Braves.

At the end of the season, the Braves and the Dodgers were tied. The pennant came down to a three-game playoff between the Braves and the Dodgers. The Braves had won the last two National League titles and were confident that they would win a third.

In the first game, the Braves took the lead, but the Dodgers came back to win. The Braves looked to have the second game won, leading 5-2 in the bottom of the ninth inning. The

Dodgers caught fire and scored three runs to tie the game. Three innings later, the Dodgers scored to win the game and the pennant. For the first time in three years, the Braves were no longer the best team in the National League. That year, Aaron won his second batting title, hitting .355. He also had 223 hits. At 25, he was the second-youngest player after Ty Cobb to reach 1,000 career hits.

Aaron was especially proud of his performance in the 1959 season. He was becoming a strong all-around hitter, the type of hitter who could make the most valuable contribution to a team. After the season, Aaron took part in a home-run competition for television that changed his outlook on hitting. The event was called the Home Run Derby. Players squared off against one another in one-on-one competition. Each home run counted as a run. Any other hit was an out. The player with the most runs after nine "innings" was the winner, and the winners took home prize money. Aaron hit plenty of homers and won about $30,000, which was nearly twice his yearly salary. Aaron began to think that he might have a future in hitting home runs. As much as he valued the all-around hitter, the home-run hitters were the ones who earned the big contracts.

A REBUILDING YEAR

The 1960 season brought a shake-up to the Braves, when the team traded some key players and changed some front-office personnel. The Braves brought in a new manager, Charlie Dressen, who had managed teams for some 20 years. Dressen was a hard-nosed guy, and the veteran players loved to see how far they could push him. The team was good enough to finish second that year in the National League, but Dressen was never in control of the Braves and was replaced partway through the 1961 season.

Over the next few years, the Braves would trade most of their reliable veterans as well as some of the most promising young players coming up through the minor leagues. They

During a game against the San Francisco Giants in May 1959, Hank Aaron hits his twelfth home run of the season. Aaron again won the batting title, with a .355 average, and he had 223 hits on the year.

finished fourth in 1961 and fifth in 1962. With fewer teammates producing runs, Aaron began to change as a hitter, focusing more on hitting the long ball. Aaron finished the 1962 season batting .323, with 128 runs batted in and 45 home runs.

As Aaron's power-hitting numbers rose, so did his salary. Home-run hitters tended to be crowd pleasers and as a result commanded the big dollars. By 1962, Aaron's annual salary was $50,000. Though the Braves were no longer serious contenders for the pennant, Aaron was reaping the rewards of the team's earlier successes as well as his own hard work. He and Barbara were enjoying their suburban home in Mequon, outside of Milwaukee, where they entertained friends and teammates at barbeques. At last, he was living the good life. His daughter Gaile, who had been staying with Aaron's parents in Mobile, moved to Milwaukee, and a new addition to the family, Dorinda, was born on February 5, 1962, Aaron's own birthday. The Aarons also had two sons, Hank and Lary. Life was good for Aaron, but after 15 years of integrated baseball, it was beginning to look better for black major leaguers in general.

THE IMPACT OF BLACK PLAYERS

By the early 1960s, it was clear that the few black players who were in the big leagues had made a tremendous impact. They had proven that baseball would not fall apart with African Americans in the game. Also, their performances on the field had taken the game to a new level. Men like Willie Mays, Ernie Banks, Roy Campanella, and Hank Aaron were the dominant players in the game. In the 1950s, black players won the National League Most Valuable Player award eight of 10 times. Over that period, black players batted a collective .280, while white players hit .261.

In the 1950s, black players made up 8 percent of all major-league players. During the 1960s, they made up 23 percent. Far more black players were in the National League than in the American League. In the National League, black players accounted for seven of ten Most Valuable Player awards in the 1960s. Seven of the 10 league batting champions in the '60s were black players or from Latin America. In that decade, black ballplayers dominated the top spots of nearly every statistical category. Despite these successes, segregation and racism remained present everywhere.

Aaron's generation was considered the second generation of black players in the major leagues. The extreme prejudice they endured carried over to the next generation as well. Black players were thrown out of restaurants, arrested by the police for no reason, and harassed by fans, who threw bottles at them and called them horrible names.

Although Major League Baseball had brought black players into the game, it had not taken the steps to create a welcoming environment. As more and more black players made major-league rosters, they began to share their stories with one another. As they talked about their experiences, they began to realize that they had the power to begin to influence change.

INTEGRATION OFF THE FIELD

One of the most significant areas of concern for black players was segregation. In many parts of the country, particularly in the South, where spring training was held, black people still had to eat in restaurant kitchens rather than in dining rooms, and they had to stay in separate hotels from their white teammates. A handful of the most prominent black players decided that they would challenge the system. They realized, though, that desegregation would be a slow process and that it would take pressure of some kind to change the minds of baseball management. So they took responsibility to bring about these changes themselves.

The St. Louis Cardinals were the first team to integrate the players' living quarters at spring training. Once they integrated, other teams would have to follow. Aaron led the way when he and other black players met with Braves general manager John McHale to discuss the matter. The result of that meeting was that all signs indicating race were removed from the ballpark in Bradenton, Florida, where the Braves played spring ball. McHale also assured the players that living facilities would be integrated during the following spring training. The problem was that the hotels in Bradenton had banded together to refuse service to black players. One hotel just outside of town, though, was not part of this arrangement, and Braves vice president Birdie Tebbetts moved all of the players there. The black players saw this as a giant step in the right direction. Still, more work needed to be done.

In 1963, the issue of race came to the forefront of the American mind. Nearly every day, one event or another that centered on race appeared on the front pages of newspapers across the United States. That summer, the Reverend Martin Luther King, Jr., led a massive demonstration in Washington, D.C., where he delivered his landmark speech, "I Have a Dream."

From that point on, race was an issue that would have to be confronted not only by African Americans but also by the entire country. As the issue became part of the collective culture, Americans responded. Many got behind Dr. King's inspiring mission, while others reacted to his powerful words with scorn and violence, as demonstrated in September 1963 with the bombing of the Sixteenth Street Baptist Church in Birmingham, Alabama, in which four young black girls were killed.

Racism was still prevalent in baseball, even in its highest office. That year, Baseball Commissioner Ford Frick made a statement about integration in baseball that had a profound effect on black players of the time. In essence, he said that black players had not been considered suitable for Major League Baseball because the game first evolved during the days of slavery, when African Americans did not have the chance to play. Black people did not start to play for another 50 years, Frick said, so it was another 50 years before they were good enough to play major-league ball.

Considering the rapid dominance of black players once they were allowed into the major leagues, Aaron was insulted by the commissioner's remarks. "What I don't understand is, if it took us 50 years to pick up a bat and another 50 years to learn how to swing it, by what miracle did we come to dominate the National League after only 10 or 15 more?" Aaron wrote in his autobiography. "The way I saw it, the commissioner's remarks were an insult to Satchel Paige and Josh Gibson and every black ballplayer who came before Jackie." It was one event that led him to swing big outside of baseball. He became more and more involved in the civil rights movement, endorsing local candidates who promoted racial equality and reading the works of the movement's prominent figures, King and James Baldwin.

THE LAST YEARS IN MILWAUKEE

In 1963, the Braves were a struggling team. No longer did they have the talent or the swagger that took them to the World Series twice in the 1950s. Aaron, however, was dominant. He hit .319 and led the league with 44 home runs, 130 runs batted in, 120 runs scored, and 370 total bases. Because the team often needed a spark, he was coached to steal bases, and he finished second in the league with 31 stolen bases in 36 attempts. The season was one of the most productive of his career. He nearly achieved the Triple Crown—he led the league in home runs and RBIs but finished third in batting average, only seven points behind the league leader. Aaron also finished third in the voting for the league's Most Valuable Player, behind Dodgers pitcher Sandy Koufax and Cardinals shortstop Dick Groat.

In 1964, the Braves looked to improve. With the addition of some young talent, the team was beginning to come together. In the Braves' restructuring, many veteran players were replaced by young up-and-comers, mainly because young players demanded lower salaries than experienced players. Nonetheless, the team finished out of the running for the pennant. Aaron had, for him, an ordinary year—his batting average was up to .328, but he only hit 24 home runs. The big news that year, though, was the team's impending move to Atlanta.

Since the glory years of the late 1950s, attendance at County Stadium had been down. As a result, the organization

★ ★ ★ ★ ★

TEAMS ON THE MOVE

The move by the Milwaukee Braves to Atlanta in 1966 was, of course, not the team's first move. The Braves had played in Boston before heading west to Milwaukee. That move, though, was the first of many in Major League Baseball to occur as teams shifted to growing cities in the Midwest, the West, and the South. Here is a list of franchises that have moved since the Boston Braves did in 1953:

Original Team	New Team	Year of Move
St. Louis Browns	Baltimore Orioles	1954
Philadelphia Athletics	Kansas City Athletics	1955
Brooklyn Dodgers	Los Angeles Dodgers	1958
New York Giants	San Francisco Giants	1958
Washington Senators	Minnesota Twins	1961
Milwaukee Braves	Atlanta Braves	1966
Kansas City Athletics	Oakland Athletics	1968
Seattle Pilots	Milwaukee Brewers	1970
Washington Senators*	Texas Rangers	1972
Montreal Expos	Washington Nationals	2005

* This Washington Senators team was founded in 1961 after the original Senators had moved to Minnesota.

Eddie Mathews and Hank Aaron were longtime teammates on the Braves, and friends as well. Both would be inducted into the Baseball Hall of Fame. They also set the major-league record for the most home runs by teammates, with 863.

was in financial straits. Management believed that a move to Atlanta would bring larger crowds, which would mean higher ticket and concessions sales. By the summer of 1964, the move seemed imminent. The city of Milwaukee, however, did not want the team to leave. A citywide movement to keep the team grew. Milwaukee's citizens even threatened to boycott Coca-Cola, whose headquarters is in Atlanta. After several battles in court, the city and county forced an injunction that kept the team in Milwaukee through the 1965 season.

In 1965, the Braves put a good team on the field. That year, Aaron and Eddie Mathews broke a record for the most home runs by two teammates. The record meant a lot to Aaron, and Mathews called it his proudest accomplishment. They broke the National League record of 745 held by Duke Snider and Gil Hodges. They thought they were still way behind the major-league record of Lou Gehrig and Babe Ruth. The record was thought to be 870 and far out of reach. As a result, the media paid little attention. Then, it was determined that, as team-mates, Gehrig and Ruth had combined for 793 home runs. And Aaron and Mathews surpassed that mark in 1965. The two Braves would go on to hit 863 home runs together.

The 1965 season would be the Braves' last one in Milwaukee. The city that had embraced the Braves when they arrived in 1953 would be left without a baseball team. But the work that Aaron and the Braves' management did to bring about change in race relations within baseball was very important to the game and to the city. It was the end of an era for Milwaukee. For Aaron, it was the beginning of a race that would consume every baseball fan in the United States.

Home
in Atlanta

Although Atlanta lacked a baseball tradition, it was the perfect city for a team like the Braves. Because the city had a larger population than Milwaukee, the potential market was larger. Also, the towns just outside of Atlanta were more heavily populated than Milwaukee's outlying areas, which were as sparsely populated as much of rural Wisconsin. Population was not all that Atlanta had going for it. It was a city on the rise and the center of progressive thinking in the South, particularly in the area of race relations.

Many of the country's best-known black thinkers lived and worked in Atlanta, including educator and civil-rights leader W.E.B. Du Bois, who taught at Atlanta University. As the home to Martin Luther King's Southern Christian Leadership Conference, Atlanta was on the forefront of the civil rights movement. Since 1961, public institutions and polling stations were integrated, and as the 1960s unfolded, Atlanta's political base became more sympathetic to racial equality. Compared with the rest of the country, let alone the rest of Georgia, Atlanta was truly progressive.

Built specifically for the Braves, Fulton County Stadium was brand new at the time. At 1,050 feet (320 meters), the stadium had the highest elevation of any baseball park in the country at the time as well as the highest average temperature. These conditions favored hitters because the ball tended to carry farther. Hank Aaron recognized a need to change his hitting style. Typically a line-drive hitter, he adjusted his swing to lift the ball higher into the air and found that it became easier to hit home runs. He also started to "pull" the ball toward left field rather than to hit it to different parts of the playing field.

On Opening Night, Aaron wanted nothing more than to hit a home run in front of the Atlanta fans who showed up to cheer their new team. It was important for him, both as a ballplayer and as a black man, to begin to build loyalty right away. He did not hit a home run that night, as the Braves lost to the Pittsburgh Pirates. He did, however, steal the first base in Fulton County Stadium history.

That season, Aaron was piling on the home runs, including No. 400 for his career. During the season, Willie Mays was approaching the National League career home-run record of 511, and reporters wanted to know if Aaron thought he could reach that number. He had hit 24 home runs so far that season, and he seemed to be making a successful transition to being a power hitter. He began to think he would have no problem hitting 500 home runs.

Hank, Barbara, and their children moved to a home with a couple of acres of property in southwest Atlanta. Despite its relatively progressive attitudes toward blacks, Atlanta and its environs remained segregated, so the Aarons' neighborhood was made up of black families. The Aarons were at first resistant to

Atlanta Braves teammates *(from left)* Felipe Alou, Joe Torre, and Hank Aaron warm up during spring training in 1968 in West Palm Beach, Florida. Fulton County Stadium, which was the Braves' new home in Atlanta, became known as a home-run-hitting park. In 1966, their first year there, Aaron, Alou, and Torre all hit more than 30 home runs apiece.

the idea of moving from Milwaukee, where they had established a comfortable home, but they soon took root in Atlanta.

All was not good, however. The Aarons received frequent reminders that, as forward-thinking a city as Atlanta might have been, it was still in the heart of Georgia. Now and again, Aaron received hate mail laced with racial insults, and at every game there were fans who hurled racial slurs at him from the stands. What kept Aaron going was the effort the Braves were making to integrate as an organization and to be a productive part of the community, a friend to both whites and blacks.

As for the team, it was exciting to watch. Aaron was joined by Joe Torre and Felipe Alou as the home-run kings of Fulton County Stadium. Each of them hit more than 30 home runs in 1966. Atlanta was getting a reputation as a good place to hit home runs. Aaron finished the season leading the league with 44 home runs and 127 runs batted in. He batted .279, though, the first season in six years he batted below .300.

SPEAKING OUT

The first years in Atlanta were productive for Aaron. He was changing as a player and as a person. As Aaron matured, he realized he would have to work harder to make his ideas and opinions heard. He began to feel that he deserved as much attention and money as anyone else in baseball. He grew angrier and more focused on achieving greatness on the field. "I was the equal of any ballplayer in the world," he recounts in *I Had a Hammer.* "And if no one was going to give me my due, it was time to grab for it."

One consequence of his newfound dedication was the deterioration of some of his personal relationships, particularly with his wife. He and Barbara seemed to have different priorities. While he wanted to focus on playing baseball and on hitting home runs, whatever the cost, Barbara wanted to raise their family in a warm home. Hank felt less and less comfortable around Barbara and began to spend more time away from home, socializing with his teammates. Like many baseball greats, Hank was the kind of player who could block out personal problems and keep on hitting. So in 1967, Aaron again led the league in home runs with 39 and in runs scored with 113, and he batted .307.

In the spring of 1968, the world seemed heavier than ever to Aaron. Just before Opening Day, Martin Luther King, Jr., was assassinated. His death was a horrible blow to the civil rights movement and to the activists who supported it. Aaron was reminded of all the good that Dr. King stood for and the role he himself had played in the civil rights movement. Dr. King had once said to a group of black baseball players that they had made his job a lot easier. Ivan Allen, the mayor of Atlanta from 1962 to 1970, said that Aaron "played a major role in smoothing the transition and confirming the end of segregation in the South through his exemplary conduct. He taught us how to do it. The first time he knocked one over that left-field fence, everyone forgot what his color was." That statement, and others like it, made Aaron feel as if he was valuable as a player and as a person. Above all else, he was proud to have helped bring Atlanta into the modern day.

Despite the death of King, the aftermath, and the mourning, baseball went on. That year, Aaron hit his 500th home run, and the Braves planned a big celebration. Aaron would be the first player of any color to have a night dedicated to him at Fulton County Stadium. It was Hank Aaron Night, and a special presentation was made to honor Aaron's achievement. Otherwise, the year was not necessarily a great one for Aaron. He hit only 29 home runs and failed to drive in 100 runs—he was pretty disappointed.

As he looked forward to the next season, he took stock of his statistics to see how he measured up to the greats. One of his goals had always been to reach 3,000 hits. Another had been to break Babe Ruth's home-run record. He figured that, at 35, he still had plenty of good hitting left. If he could play and keep his production up for another few years, he could be an all-time leader in several categories, including hits, home runs, total bases, and runs batted in. His average of .314 was also the highest of any current player at the time, so he knew he stood a good chance of finishing his career high on the list of all-time leaders.

"To somebody like me," Aaron wrote in *I Had a Hammer*, "having come along in a period when black players were only beginning to assume their rightful place in baseball—the chance to make history sounded like something worth pursuing with all of my resources."

Aaron knew something else, too. He was well aware of the fans' perception of him. For most of his career, people had thought of him as a simpleminded, almost lazy player who, although he was talented, lacked the charisma of the game's greatest players, like Willie Mays, Roberto Clemente, or Babe Ruth. He realized that he did not capture the hearts of fans like most of the other players. A look at his career numbers, however, showed that he was among the league leaders every season he played. He knew he was one of the game's better players. Aaron also knew, though, that if he were to be remembered, he would have to surpass the other great players statistically. And that goal was within sight, as long as his body held up.

Aaron was always known as someone who played in a way that was easy on his body. By that point in his career, however, he suffered bone chips in his back and other ailments that caused him quite a bit of pain. As the years wore on, he could be seen limping around the clubhouse, stooped over in pain. As soon as he walked onto the field, though, he stood up straight and played the game like a young man.

The 1969 season was business as usual for Aaron, but the Braves were playing high-caliber baseball. Following the mid-season break for the All-Star Game, the Braves were part of a four-way battle with the Dodgers, Giants, and Reds for supremacy in the National League West. (In 1969, both leagues added two teams and split into East and West divisions.) The Braves figured that the winner would play the Cubs for the pennant, but the Mets came on strong and stole the National League East title from the faltering Cubs.

Meanwhile, the Braves clinched their division near the end of September after winning 10 consecutive games. The Mets

Hank Aaron slides into second during a game in 1969 against the New York Mets. That season, Aaron and the Braves played in the post-season for the first time in 11 years—also against the Mets. New York swept Atlanta to win the National League Championship Series.

had won 100 games that year on the strength of their pitching staff, which included Jerry Koosman and Tom Seaver, and they proved to be the better team. Although Aaron hit a home run in each game, the Mets swept the Braves in three games in the National League Championship Series. New York went on to win the World Series over the Baltimore Orioles.

(*continues on page 74*)

☆ ☆ ☆ ☆ ☆

BABE RUTH

In the early 1970s, people began to consider the possibility that Hank Aaron might break Babe Ruth's career home-run record. Ruth was the symbol of big-league baseball, and many consider him to be the greatest baseball player of all time. His excellent record, first as a pitcher and later as a hitter, is testament to his athleticism and versatility. At the time, no one had a bigger influence on how baseball would be played in the future than Ruth.

George Herman Ruth was born on February 6, 1895, in Baltimore, Maryland. At the age of seven, he was sent by his parents to a school for boys. As a child, he was something of a delinquent, skipping school, chewing tobacco, and drinking alcohol. At the school, though, he learned the game of baseball. He played catcher as a youngster and began to pitch when he was 15. Ruth signed on to a minor-league team, the Baltimore Orioles, in 1914, and later his contract was sold to the major leagues' Boston Red Sox. As a pitcher, Ruth was dominant. In 1916, he was the best pitcher in the league, with an ERA of 1.75 and a record of 23–12. The next year, he hit .325, and his coaches decided that he would be more valuable to the team as a hitter.

From 1915 to 1918, the Red Sox won three World Series, with plenty of help from Ruth. In 1919, though, the team fell to sixth place in the American League. Ruth's drinking binges and his free-wheeling lifestyle were considered problems, and he had frequent run-ins with the Red Sox coaching staff. In what has become baseball's most legendary trade, the Red Sox sold Ruth to the New York Yankees. In 1920, his first season with

the Yankees, Ruth shattered the season record of 29 home runs,
which he held, by hitting 54 home runs.

Ruth became an icon in 1920s New York, the center
of the "Swinging '20s." He dated a lot of women, drank a
lot of liquor, and ate a lot of food. New Yorkers loved him,
and attendance at the Polo Grounds increased so dramati-
cally that the team built a new, larger stadium called Yankee
Stadium. It also became known as "The House That Ruth Built."
During the 1927 and 1928 seasons, Ruth played on Yankees
teams that were thought to be the best ever and part of a larger
dynasty that is considered one of the greatest in all of sports.

Ruth's effect on the game was profound. At the time, the
common hitting style was to choke up on the bat and take short,
compact swings. This enabled hitters to make contact with the
ball more easily, but their hits were shorter. In contrast, Ruth took
huge, wide swings, hitting the ball hard and far when he made
contact. Most hitters today favor Ruth's style, mainly because
home runs are considered such an important part of the game.

Ruth played with the Yankees through the 1934 season.
He joined the Boston Braves in 1935, but played only one season for them. When he retired, he held the career home-run
record, with 714. The following year, he was one of the first
five players elected to the Baseball Hall of Fame. He spent his
years after baseball giving talks on the radio and at orphanages
and hospitals. After many ups and downs, Ruth died of cancer
at age 53. He remains the greatest legend in the history
of baseball.

(*continued from page 71*)

A MAJOR MILESTONE: 3,000 HITS

A baseball player has to have two qualities to reach the rare mark of 3,000 career hits: He has to have the skills to put the bat on the ball, and he has to have longevity. Some of the greatest hitters in baseball never joined the 3,000-hit club because they rapidly lost their skills as they aged or their careers were interrupted or cut short by injury. In 1970, eight players had 3,000 hits: Ty Cobb, Stan Musial, Eddie Collins, Tris Speaker, Honus Wagner, Napoleon Lajoie, Cap Anson, and Paul Waner. Of those eight, only Musial had played after World War II.

Aaron had proven he could hit the ball. Early in his career, he was known for hitting line drives all over the field. He had also never missed much time because of injuries. Later in his career, particularly when the Braves moved to Atlanta, he changed his batting style to allow for more home runs. Because he swung under the ball to lift it higher toward the outfield fence, he had fewer base hits. Still, the hits did keep coming, and on May 17, 1970, in Cincinnati, after 16 seasons in the major leagues, Aaron hit No. 3,000, and it was a big moment for him, for African Americans, and for all of baseball.

When the team returned to Atlanta, the Braves held a special day to honor Aaron's achievement. Among the somewhat odd selection of gifts Aaron received were the ball with which he hit his big hit, a golf cart, and a poodle. The moment was a proud one for Aaron, but there was more baseball to play. That same season, Willie Mays got his 3,000th hit. Aaron always thought of his friend as a competitor, and he was doubly proud to have reached the milestone first.

Mays had about 40 more career home runs than Aaron at this time, so any talk of breaking Babe Ruth's record focused on Mays. Aaron, though, was still thinking he had a chance. He had Ruth's record in sight, but it would not be easy. There would be many challenges along the way.

As Aaron focused more and more on hitting home runs, his life at home suffered even more. Barbara Aaron filed for divorce, and Hank Aaron, unable to believe that they could

Hank Aaron follows through after getting the 3,000th hit of his career on May 17, 1970, at Cincinnati. The Braves held a special celebration for Aaron when they returned to Atlanta. After reaching this milestone, Aaron began to focus on the possibility of breaking Babe Ruth's home-run record.

not reconcile, moved into an apartment downtown. It was an especially troubling time for Aaron. He worried about how the divorce would affect their children. He grew sad and lonesome, admitting that he was not cut out for the single life. Still, he kept his mission in the front of his mind. If he was to be remembered as not only one of the best black baseball players of all time, but as one of the best players of any race, he would have to start producing more home runs, regardless of the toll his quest took on his personal life.

Home-Run
Champion

Hank Aaron's low spirits carried over into the next season. He saw his children on a regular basis, driving them to school and spending time with them after school when he could. But he missed having them around him when he was home. Living on his own was painful, but he was driven to reach his potential as a hitter. If he was to focus on his mission, he would just have to make some sacrifices.

The 1971 season came and went. Statistically, Aaron had what had become an average year for him. He was putting up the same steady numbers, but his body was growing tired from the wear and tear, and he had lost a step on the base paths. Yet he remained one of the best all-around players and home-run hitters in the game. Also, people were beginning to realize in 1971 that Aaron might have a shot at breaking Babe Ruth's record.

Before spring training in 1972, he signed a two-year contract that at the time was thought to be outrageous. He became the first player to earn more than $200,000 a season. Although he was pleased with his contract, fans criticized him for being greedy. Because his salary was significantly higher than most white players, racists had yet another reason to attack him. Aaron's performance in the early part of the season gave critics plenty to yell about. He was striking out more frequently than usual, although his home-run production remained even. In June, he hit his 649th home run, moving him into second place, ahead of Willie Mays, who was still playing, on the list of top home-run hitters. At the halfway point of the season, his 660th home run broke the record for the most home runs by someone playing for a single team. Aaron was proud of this accomplishment because it recognized his contribution to the team. He was not finished, however, with setting records that year.

In September, against the Philadelphia Phillies, Aaron hit two home runs and broke the record for career total bases held by Stan Musial. Aaron was especially proud of this record. To him, the total bases statistic was the most accurate measure of a hitter's success. He thought that the record reflected the kind of all-around hitter he was, particularly earlier in his career. Aaron also respected Musial as a person and was happy to be in his company as a hitter and as a representative of baseball. "If there is any one record that I think best represents what I was all about as a hitter, that's the one, because as far as I was concerned, the object of batting was to hit the ball and get as many bases as possible."

By now it was apparent to the Braves' management that Aaron would almost certainly break Ruth's home-run record at some point in the near future. Aaron was already receiving an enormous amount of fan mail, and the Braves anticipated that it would only increase as Aaron closed in on the record. They assigned him a personal secretary, who would assist him with his mail and with public relations, including scheduling interviews with magazines, newspapers, and television shows. They hoped the secretary would take some pressure off Aaron and allow him to focus on playing ball.

A NEW COMPANION

As the 1972 season wore on, Aaron began to find his groove again. This time, it was not baseball that put a spring in his step; setting new records was something he expected. Instead, it was the people in his life—two in particular. The first was an old friend; the second, a new friend. His old pal and teammate Eddie Mathews was hired as the Braves' new manager. It was only when Mathews arrived that Aaron realized he had missed

☆ ☆ ☆ ☆ ☆

CAREER TOTAL-BASES LEADERS

Rank	Player	Total Bases (as of 2006)
1	Hank Aaron	6,856
2	Stan Musial	6,134
3	Willie Mays	6,066
4	Ty Cobb	5,854
5	Babe Ruth	5,793
6	Barry Bonds*	5,784
7	Pete Rose	5,752
8	Carl Yastrzemski	5,539
9	Eddie Murray	5,397
10	Rafael Palmeiro	5,388

* still active

After his divorce, Hank Aaron met Billye Williams when he appeared on her television talk show in Atlanta. Williams is pictured here at a Braves game in the early 1970s. A former English instructor at Atlanta University, Williams introduced Aaron to some of the most prominent civil rights activists in the nation.

being around his old teammates day in and day out. Most of the players on the team were younger, and Aaron frequently found himself playing the role of mentor. He longed for the camaraderie that players of his generation offered. Mathews was just the fix.

The new person who came into Aaron's life was a morning talk-show host named Billye Williams. She was the co-host of a show in Atlanta called *Today in Georgia*. Billye's husband, Sam Williams, had died in 1970. A well-known activist in the civil rights movement, Sam Williams had been a pastor as well as a professor at Morehouse College, but he was best known as "the voice of reason" in Atlanta, serving as an intermediary between black activists and the white community. Martin Luther King had been one of his students. Billye Williams met Aaron when her show planned a series on baseball personalities. Aaron was to be the first of her interviews. Aaron asked her out to dinner, but she refused, saying she was not ready to be seen dating in public. Aaron understood, but he was not going to give up.

The two began to spend time together out of the public eye. Williams had been an English teacher at Atlanta University and introduced Aaron to a world he had only sampled. Although Aaron had strong opinions about race relations and had the opportunity to befriend some of the movement's better-known activists, he wanted to do more. Because he was interviewed for television shows and magazine articles so often, he had plenty of chances to express his views.

He felt somewhat awkward, though. Williams introduced him to books and ideas that helped him shape and articulate his thoughts. This was exactly what Aaron had craved. It was as if he had known, all during his career, that he was destined to make contributions to society of more value than his contributions on the baseball diamond. Now he was beginning to fully realize his role and his ability to deliver.

Aaron began to think about how he could play a bigger role in black society. He organized a charity bowling tournament to raise money to fight sickle cell anemia, a serious disease that is more prevalent among black people. The tournament included some of baseball's best players. Aaron was thrilled to make a contribution. "It was my first tangible dividend for hitting home runs," he said in *I Had a Hammer*.

At the end of the day, though, baseball was his calling, and the home-run record was in his sights. Aaron belted 34 home runs in 1972, leaving him 41 shy of Ruth's record. He had hit more than 40 home runs a season plenty of times, but he was getting older and did not think he would be able to break the record the next year. Aaron was so close that the record was weighing heavily on his mind.

AS CLOSE AS IT GETS

He was motivated by several factors. First, like any ballplayer, Aaron wanted to break records, especially such a highly regarded, long-standing mark. Second, he had always believed he never got the recognition as a player that he deserved—if he broke the record, no one could dispute his talent and contribution to the game. Third, he would undoubtedly receive some financial reward for setting the new record, either from the Braves or from endorsements. And fourth, Aaron had a chance to accomplish something for his race. He had always

★ ★ ★ ★ ★ ☆

CAREER RBI LEADERS

Rank	Player	RBIs (as of 2006)
1	Hank Aaron	2,297
2	Babe Ruth	2,217
3	Cap Anson	2,076
4	Lou Gehrig	1,995
5	Stan Musial	1,951
6	Ty Cobb	1,937
7	Barry Bonds*	1,930
8	Jimmie Foxx	1,922
9	Eddie Murray	1,917
10	Willie Mays	1,903

* still active

wanted to contribute to activism and to the civil rights movement, and given his talents, the home-run record was his unique way of showing the world that black people are as important as white people.

To that end, he had a strong desire to build on the work his hero Jackie Robinson had begun. Robinson had recently died, and Aaron felt responsible for doing all he could to honor the man. "It made me more determined than ever to keep Jackie's dream alive, and the best way I could do that was to become the all-time home run champion in the history of the game that had kept out black people for more than 60 years. I owed it to Jackie."

Aaron was more than eager to begin the 1973 season. His life was coming back together. He had Billye Williams's support. His old friend Eddie Mathews was calling the shots from the dugout. And the home-run record was within sight. One way or another, it was looking like an exciting season. Aaron was so close to breaking the most heralded record in baseball he could almost taste it. He was in for a rude awakening, though. At 39, he was old by baseball standards.

Plenty of fans and reporters felt that Aaron was hanging around only so he could have a shot at breaking the record. Early in the season, Aaron threw fuel on the fire by usually hitting home runs or striking out. His batting average hovered around .200. Suddenly, an uproar broke out over his motivation. People thought he was no longer hitting for the Braves but only for the record. Fans at the ballpark expressed their outrage with verbal tirades. He received hundreds of letters criticizing his character. Aaron was surprised and disheartened. He was excited about the home run chase, and he expected the fans to support him in his quest to break the record.

Because of his aching body, Aaron was playing only two-thirds of the games. Some said he looked like an old man between innings. Every time he came up to bat or took the field, though, he looked as fresh as he had 10 years before.

Hank Aaron watches the flight of the ball after he hit his 700th career home run against the Philadelphia Phillies on July 21, 1973. Two months remained in the season, and it appeared that Aaron would have a good shot to break Babe Ruth's record that year.

Nonetheless, his throwing arm had grown weak enough that Mathews moved him from right field to left field.

On top of it all, Aaron was receiving bags full of hate mail every day as he came closer and closer to the record. The letters, some 3,000 per day, were filled with abusive comments about his race. Worse still, they included threats to him and to his family. The letters motivated Aaron, but they also made life difficult for him. It came to the point that the FBI was confiscating letters and tracking down the people who wrote them. Aaron's daughter, Gaile, was a target of a kidnapping that never transpired. The threats got so bad that the Braves and the city assigned a policeman to follow Aaron.

Through all of the distractions, Aaron kept on hitting. He slammed his 700th home run in mid-July, and the possibility of his reaching Ruth's record of 714 that season was becoming more and more real. The summer heat in Atlanta, however, began to take its toll on Aaron, and his performance started to taper off. What did not slow down was the media attention. When he was not in the batter's box, he was almost constantly besieged by reporters and interviewers. He had never been more popular. His picture appeared on the cover of *Newsweek*. He received offers to appear on television dramas and soap operas.

Everyone, it seemed, wanted a piece of him. Yet somehow the fans in Atlanta remained cool to the spectacle. Attendance at the Braves' home games was way down. Aaron could not understand why that would be when one of the team's players was chasing the most important record in baseball.

By the last series of the regular season, Aaron had hit 712 home runs—only two shy of tying the record. The Braves had a three-game homestand against the Houston Astros, and all of baseball eagerly waited to see if Aaron would match Ruth. Aaron went hitless in the first game but delivered a homer in the second. It came down to the final game of the season. The first time he batted, he hit a single. He came up again and singled again. He singled at his third at-bat. And on his fourth and last at-bat of the season, he hit a shallow fly ball that was caught by an infielder. Aaron batted three-for-four that day, but he did not hit the home run that would tie Ruth's record. He would have to wait until the next season. To his surprise, Aaron was treated to a standing ovation after his last at-bat. It looked as if Atlanta's fans were behind him after all.

Considering how poorly his season had started, Hank pulled it together and had a pretty good year. He hit 40 home runs, or one home run every 10 at-bats. He also drove in just under 100 runs and hit .301. He had not, though, hit home run No. 714, and it would be several months before he stepped onto the field again.

THE SEASON OPENS

Aaron had enough to keep his mind off the record. Just after the season ended, he was approached by Magnavox, a maker of electronics, and offered the job of being its spokesman. The offer meant doing a few TV commercials or magazine advertisements. For the most part, it meant he was giving the company permission to use his name when they talked about its products. Aaron was to be paid $1 million for being the spokesman. At the time, the money was the most that any professional athlete had made to endorse a product.

In November 1973, he and Billye Williams were married. Aaron was happy at last to have found a companion and to settle back into family life. (Billye had a daughter, Ceci, whom Aaron adopted.) There was not always much time for home life, however. Aaron spent most of the off-season delivering talks at banquets all over the country. He also did more than a few guest appearances on television shows, like Flip Wilson's and Dean Martin's variety shows and Dinah Shore's and Merv Griffin's talk shows. Aaron kept so busy that he was able to put the home-run chase behind him, though in the back of his mind he was ready for Opening Day.

When Aaron reported to spring training in 1974, he learned that the Braves wanted to keep him out of the first three road games so he could break Ruth's record in Atlanta. Bowie Kuhn, the commissioner of baseball, did not think that was fair. He ordered the Braves to play Aaron in at least two of the three games. By then, Aaron was ready to break the record. He was weary of all of the attention and of the constant presence of reporters in the clubhouse and stadium parking lot. It was time to get it done and move on.

Aaron was in the lineup on Opening Day against the Cincinnati Reds. He would play that game and one of the remaining two before going back to Atlanta. On Opening Day, Aaron had some business to take care of before the game. It was the anniversary of Martin Luther King's assassination, and Aaron requested that there be a moment of silence to pay tribute to the memory of the great activist. When the team took batting practice, throngs of reporters surrounded Aaron, asking him how he felt and if he thought he could tie the Babe that day. Aaron was gracious, but he could not wait to play ball.

Finally, the game began. He came up to bat with two men on base. With the count at three balls and one strike, he took his first swing of the 1974 season, connecting with the ball and sending it flying over the fence. He had just tied Babe Ruth on the list of all-time home runs. The entire Braves bench cleared and ran to home plate to congratulate Aaron. He went to the stands and hugged his father and Billye, and he shook Vice President Gerald Ford's hand. It was a huge moment for everyone. And Aaron had only one more home run to hit to break the record. He sat out the next game, and in the third game he had trouble with the pitcher, striking out twice and grounding out. He would have to wait for Atlanta after all.

THE BIG SWING

The Braves' home opener against the Los Angeles Dodgers was a spectacle. The stadium was packed with 54,000 fans for a special Hank Aaron Night. Marching bands and cannons added to the racket. Truth be told, the Braves had planned this night some time ago, thinking Aaron would have already broken the record. For Aaron and the fans, it just added to the fun. Aaron's old coaches and friends were in the crowd. So were some notable fans, including Jimmy Carter, the governor of Georgia and future president of the United States. One man who was not there was Baseball Commissioner Bowie Kuhn,

Hank Aaron holds up the ball he hit to break Babe Ruth's home-run record. Aaron belted his 715th homer in a game on April 8, 1974, against the Los Angeles Dodgers. During a short ceremony after his home run, Aaron said, "Thank God it's over."

who had ordered Aaron to play in Cincinnati. Aaron took Kuhn's absence as a personal insult.

The Dodgers put Al Downing on the mound. The first time Aaron came to bat, the crowd went wild, and flashbulbs went off all over the stadium as fans snapped pictures. He was walked and scored when Dusty Baker hit a double. That run moved Aaron into third place and past Willie Mays on the list of career runs scored. Aaron came up again in the fourth inning, and that was when he made history, taking the second pitch over the fence and into the record books. He had hit more

☆ ☆ ☆ ☆ ☆ ☆

CAREER HOME-RUN LEADERS

Rank	Player	Home Runs (as of 2006)
1	Barry Bonds*	760
2	Hank Aaron	755
3	Babe Ruth	714
4	Willie Mays	660
5	Sammy Sosa*	604
6	Ken Griffey, Jr.*	590
7	Frank Robinson	586
8	Mark McGwire	583
9	Harmon Killebrew	573
10	Rafael Palmeiro*	569

* still active

home runs than anyone in the history of baseball. He was the Home Run King.

As Aaron circled the bases, the Dodger infielders congratulated him, and two excited young men jumped out of the stands to run beside him. Aaron could hardly believe this was the moment he had been working toward his whole career. "I was in my own little world at the time," he wrote in his autobiography about rounding the bases after the home run. "It was like I was running in a bubble and I could see all these people jumping up and down and waving their arms in slow motion. I remember that every base seem crowded, like there were all these people I had to get through to make it to home plate. I just couldn't wait to get there."

The game was stopped for a brief ceremony, during which Aaron quipped into the microphone, "Thank God it's over." Later Aaron would tell an interviewer, "When I hit the ball that night, I knew it had a chance to go out. The only thing that worried me that evening was if I hit it in the stands, somebody was going to catch it and eventually put it in a vault and try to sell it for megabucks. But that didn't happen. It was given back to me, and that ball and bat are in Turner Field. God works in mysterious ways. He saw fit that Tom House caught the ball, and House brought it back to me. The thing I'm so proud of is that my mother and my father were there. My father is no longer with us. It was a great night all the way."

The Braves went on to win the game. Afterward, manager Eddie Mathews closed the clubhouse doors to everyone but ballplayers and their families. The sportswriters were left outside. Champagne was brought out. Mathews had the team gather around him for a toast, and he told the players that he thought Aaron was the best baseball player he had ever known. It was a special moment for Aaron, hearing such kind words from his friend—the perfect way to end a record-setting night.

Hank Aaron played his final two seasons in the city where his major-league career began—Milwaukee. He was a designated hitter for the Milwaukee Brewers. Now in his 40s, though, he struggled at the plate. Aaron finished his career with 755 home runs and 2,297 runs batted in, also a major-league record.

A CAREER WINDING DOWN

Hank Aaron would play through the 1976 season, when he retired as a Milwaukee Brewer. (Milwaukee had regained a major-league team in 1970, when the expansion Seattle Pilots moved to the Wisconsin city.) Aaron was traded to the team before the start of the 1975 season. He was returning to the city where his major-league career began. "The trade wasn't a complete surprise to me . . . but it was news, and great news," Aaron wrote in *I Had a Hammer.* "I still loved Milwaukee . . . and Milwaukee still loved me. I knew I would be going to a place where I was wanted, and that sounded awfully good."

Since he was now in the American League, Aaron was used as the team's designated hitter. Being in a different league, though, also meant that the pitchers were unfamiliar to him. Aaron struggled during the 1975 season, batting only .234 with 12 home runs. He played in about half the games in 1976 and did not do much better at the plate. "There was no mistaking it—I couldn't go on another year," Aaron wrote in his autobiography. "I knew it was over when I couldn't hit consistently in batting practice." His final home run came on July 20, 1976, against the California Angels—his tenth of the season and the 755th of his career.

Over 23 seasons, he played in 3,298 games. He batted 12,364 times and had 3,771 hits. He scored 2,174 runs and batted in 2,297 runs. His career RBI total continues to stand as a major-league record. With his 755 home runs, he would be remembered by fans as the Home Run King. But he would be remembered by baseball men as something else: the best example of a total hitter baseball had ever seen and a player who was such a complete all-around hitter that he just happened to hit enough home runs to dethrone the legendary "Sultan of Swat," Babe Ruth.

Others will remember Aaron as the brave young man who paved the way for African Americans to play minor-league ball in the Deep South. They will remember how he withstood the humiliating racial taunts of the stadium crowds, how he stewed in silence when he was refused service at a restaurant because he was not white, and how he stood up to thousands upon thousands of hate letters while pursuing a record that would become his way of showing the world that the color of a person's skin had no bearing on his character.

A Life
After Baseball

As with all aging stars of major-league sports, the time comes when their careers as players give way to other careers. After spending many years playing baseball, many players find the transition to "ordinary" life difficult. This is true of baseball players as well. The daily routine of drills, games, and travel over the course of nine months each year leaves time for little else. When retirement arrives, many stars are left with a void that is hard to fill.

For Hank Aaron, though, no such void existed. Throughout his playing days, baseball came first. As he matured, he was quick to realize that there were other important parts of life. He knew that, at the end of such a standout career, he could take advantage of his baseball knowledge and his celebrity to create opportunities that could be just as fulfilling as the game he so dearly loved. He was respected as a team leader, and he was adored by the Braves' management for bringing the team the career home-run record. The African-American community looked to him as an example of civil-rights success, and to baseball fans of all ages across the country, he was a hero.

Aaron spent his early post-playing career managing the personal connections he had established as a player. His heart was still in the game, and immediately after his retirement as a player, Aaron went to work for the Braves in a different capacity. In 1976, Ted Turner, who would start the CNN news network, bought the Braves. Turner had contacted Aaron about coming back to the team, and he appointed Aaron to run the Braves' six-team farm system. After developing a thorough understanding of the farm system and getting to know the coaches, scouts, and players, he was promoted to vice president of player development. With this new position, he became one of the first black executives in Major League Baseball. His overseeing of young talent—like Dale Murphy, who was named the National League Most Valuable Player in 1982 and 1983—was instrumental in the Braves winning the National League West in 1982. Since 1989, he has served the Braves as senior vice president and assistant to the president. He serves on the team's Board of Directors, playing a part in all of the organization's major decisions. Aaron is also involved in several community-relations roles with the city of Atlanta and has become a leading spokesman for minority hiring in baseball.

"They've never given us an opportunity to do anything other than play between the two white lines," Aaron said in a 1987 interview with the *Washington Post*. "I feel that, if I had not ended up with 755 home runs, and let people know that I was interested in working with the minor-league system, I would probably be as ousted as anyone else right now."

Hank Aaron *(right)*, Frank Robinson *(center)*, and Albert "Happy" Chandler celebrate their induction into the Baseball Hall of Fame in August 1982. Robinson was a star outfielder and the first black manager of a major-league team. Chandler was the commissioner of baseball when Jackie Robinson first entered the major leagues.

THE HALL OF FAME

Aaron continued to receive awards and honors long after his career had ended. In 1982, he was given the most prestigious honor in all of baseball when he was inducted into the Baseball Hall of Fame. The Hall of Fame is a museum in Cooperstown, New York, that celebrates baseball's greatest players. Players who have 10 years of major-league experience are eligible for the Hall of Fame five years after their retirement. Each year, about 25 to 40 players are nominated for selection. From this group, members of the Baseball Writers' Association of America vote for up to 10 players. Any player who is named on 75 percent or more of all ballots is elected to the Hall of Fame. Several of the game's outstanding players are nominated year after year and are never voted into the Hall of Fame. Aaron, though, was selected in the first year he was eligible. He was named on 97.8 percent of the ballots (only 9 of 415 voters did not select him), second only to Ty Cobb, who received votes on 98.2 percent of the ballots in 1936.

Being elected to the Hall of Fame was a fitting honor that capped his amazing career as a hitter and multiple winner of the Gold Glove award. It was also a fitting honor for one of the first players to break baseball's color barrier. During his induction speech in Cooperstown, Aaron acknowledged the great teachers from whom he had learned about the game of baseball and about survival as a black celebrity in a racist world. He paid special thanks to his wife and his children, whom he credits for their support throughout his career.

The National Baseball Hall of Fame and Museum features exhibits honoring Aaron and his breaking of the career home run record. A plaque honoring each of the inductees appears in the Hall of Fame, detailing the player's career highlights. Aaron's plaque reads as follows:

HENRY "HANK" L. AARON
MILWAUKEE N.L., ATLANTA N.L.,
MILWAUKEE A.L., 1954–1976
Hit 755 home runs in 23-year career to become majors'
all-time homer king. Had 20 or more for 20 consecutive
years, at least 30 in 15 seasons, and 40 or better eight times.
Also set records for games played (3,298), at-bats (12,364),
long hits (1,477), total bases (6,856), runs batted in (2,297).
Paced N.L. in batting twice and homers, runs batted in
and slugging pct. four times each. Won Most
Valuable Player award in N.L. in 1957.

The Atlanta Braves honored Aaron by inducting him into the organization's Hall of Fame and by retiring his number. The Milwaukee Brewers also retired Aaron's number. And both teams have erected statues of Aaron outside the front entrances of Turner Field, where the Braves now play in Atlanta, and Miller Park, where the Brewers now play in Milwaukee.

In 1999, Aaron was named to baseball's All-Century Team. A panel of experts had compiled a list of the 100 greatest players from the twentieth century. Fans then voted on their choices from that list. The top two infielders, top six pitchers, and top nine outfielders made the team. Aaron received the third-most votes of all players, behind only Lou Gehrig and Babe Ruth. Also that year, he was ranked No. 5 by *Sporting News* among the 100 Greatest Baseball Players.

IN BUSINESS

Even while he was playing, Aaron thought ahead to life after baseball. He realized that a person with his public appeal would have an advantage in the business world, and he began to foster relationships with several entrepreneurs in preparation for the day when he could build his own business. During his playing days, Aaron developed a friendship with Frank Belatti, an executive with Arby's restaurants. Under Belatti's guidance, Aaron purchased an Arby's franchise in Milwaukee. "Frank Belatti has been extremely fathering to me," Aaron said in an interview. "I tell all athletes to make valuable contacts when you're playing baseball. In this situation, the people I made contact with eventually came back to me to get into business." Once he had successfully established the first restaurant, he bought more, eventually owning seven Arby's franchises. His involvement in the restaurant business grew as he became more experienced. At one point, he owned 19 restaurants, including Church's, Popeye's, and Krispy Kreme, all of which he sold as he grew older.

Aaron also established contacts that would help him start several automobile dealerships. The first was a BMW dealership that opened in December 1999 in Union City, Georgia. He opened several others, using his name to promote the dealerships. The success of these businesses, though, was due to much more than Aaron's celebrity. The automobile dealerships became famous for their spotless cleanliness and their no-pressure sales staff. Aaron established an office at the BMW dealership so he could interact with his customers and make sure they were well treated.

Aaron has also been involved in other businesses and institutions in Atlanta. He has served as vice president and a member of the Board of Directors of the Turner Broadcasting System, Ted Turner's large media company. He was the vice president for business development for the Airport Channel. He also served on the National Board of the NAACP and the Sterling Committee of Morehouse College in Atlanta.

LIFETIME RECOGNITION

Since he stepped off the diamond as player, Aaron has developed a strong reputation for giving back to society. One such venture includes a charitable foundation he created to help youngsters. Aaron established the Chasing the Dream Foundation to help children between the ages of nine and 12 realize their dreams just as he realized his. The foundation gives grants to children to enable them to advance their study of music, art, writing, dance, and sports.

Aaron's accomplishments on and off the field continue to be commemorated later in his life. At his sixty-fifth birthday celebration in Atlanta on February 5, 1999, Aaron was honored for his lifetime achievements as a player and as a humanitarian. President Bill Clinton, Baseball Commissioner Bud Selig, and Chicago Cubs star Sammy Sosa were among those in attendance as Major League Baseball recognized Aaron's talents with the introduction of the Hank Aaron Award. The award, unveiled at

Hank Aaron blows out the candles on a cake shaped like Fulton County Stadium during his sixty-fifth birthday celebration in February 1999. Among the baseball greats attending the party were *(from left)* Reggie Jackson, Frank Robinson, Sammy Sosa, Don Baylor, Phil Niekro, Sonny Jackson, and Ernie Banks. At the birthday celebration, Major League Baseball announced the creation of the Hank Aaron Award.

the 1999 World Series, is presented annually to honor the best hitters in the National and American Leagues.

On July 9, 2002, Aaron was named a recipient of the Presidential Medal of Freedom, the nation's highest civilian honor. During the ceremony, President George W. Bush said of Aaron: "Hank Aaron overcame poverty and racism to become one of the most accomplished baseball players of all time. . . . By steadily pursuing his calling in the face of unreasoning hatred, Hank Aaron has proved himself a great human being, as well as a great athlete."

☆ ☆ ☆ ☆ ☆

THE HANK AARON AWARD

On February 5, 1999—Hank Aaron's sixty-fifth birthday—Major League Baseball Commissioner Bud Selig announced the creation of the Hank Aaron Award, to honor the best overall offensive performer in the National and American Leagues. The award was introduced to honor the twenty-fifth anniversary of Aaron's setting of a new career home-run record. It was the first major award to be created in more than 30 years and the first award named after a player who is still alive. The award serves to commemorate Aaron's prowess as a complete hitter.

In the award's first year, the winners were chosen by a point system. Hits, home runs, and RBIs were given certain point values, and the players with the most points won the award. The system changed the following year. The radio and TV announcers for each ball club vote for whom they consider to be the top three offensive players in each league. The first-place vote gets five points; the second-place vote, three points; and the third-place vote, one point. The player with the most points wins the Hank Aaron Award. Starting in 2003, fans had the chance to vote on the award through the MLB.com Web site. Fan voting counted for 30 percent of the points, with the announcers' voting counting for the rest.

Alex Rodriguez and Barry Bonds have each won the award three times. Other recipients include Derek Jeter, Albert Pujols, and Sammy Sosa.

A few months later, in February 2003, Aaron received the first Jackie Robinson Lifetime Achievement Legacy Award from the Negro Leagues Baseball Museum, honoring his "career excellence in the face of adversity." The museum, in Kansas City, Missouri, is dedicated to preserving the history of African Americans in baseball.

Despite his successful business ventures, Aaron's interests remain in baseball and in civil rights and racial equality, particularly behind the closed doors of Major League Baseball's executive world. "Henry assumes a level of responsibility for the community," said Jesse Jackson, the civil-rights activist and one-time presidential candidate, in a 1987 *Washington Post* article. "And, among athletes, that is rare." Aaron continues to fight for integration in the front offices of baseball teams across the country, so that future generations of African Americans will not have to play only between the white lines.

A PIONEER'S LEGACY

Hank Aaron took his place in history as the man who broke Babe Ruth's long-standing career home-run record. But his impression on America is deeper and broader. From his start as a cross-handed-hitting shortstop for the Indianapolis Clowns of the Negro American League, Aaron was thrust into a position of great responsibility. As a black athlete in white America, he faced racism and fought back. Sent to the South Atlantic League to help integrate baseball in the Deep South, he stood his ground against hatred and controversy and helped to open the doors to younger black players across the country.

His career was the stuff of dreams. He set all-time records for home runs and total bases and RBIs, and earned two batting titles and three Gold Gloves. He was the hero of the 1957 World Series. Following his career as a player, Aaron assumed influential positions in the front office of the Atlanta Braves organization. In this role, he was an unofficial spokesman for racial concerns around Major League Baseball.

After a Hall of Fame career and countless contributions to baseball and to the Atlanta community, now more than anything Aaron enjoys spending time with his wife, children, and grandchildren in Atlanta. As San Francisco Giants slugger Barry Bonds approaches Aaron's home-run total, Aaron may not worry about the day the record will be broken. After all, his legacy reaches far beyond the baseball diamond.

STATISTICS

HANK AARON

Primary position: Right field
(also CF; LF; 1B; DH)

Full name: Henry Louis Aaron •
Born: February 5, 1934, Mobile, Alabama •
Height: 6'0" Weight: 180 lbs. •
Teams: Milwaukee Braves (1954–1965);
Atlanta Braves (1966–1974); Milwaukee
Brewers (1975–1976)

☆ ☆ ☆ ☆ ☆ ☆

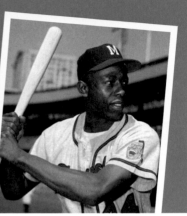

YEAR	TEAM	G	AB	H	HR	RBI	BA
1954	MLN	122	468	131	13	69	.280
1955	MLN	153	602	189	27	106	.314
1956	MLN	153	609	200	26	92	.328
1957	MLN	151	615	198	44	132	.322
1958	MLN	153	601	196	30	95	.326
1959	MLN	154	629	223	39	123	.355
1960	MLN	153	590	172	40	126	.292
1961	MLN	155	603	197	34	120	.327
1962	MLN	156	592	191	45	128	.323
1963	MLN	161	631	201	44	130	.319
1964	MLN	145	570	187	24	95	.328
1965	MLN	150	570	181	32	89	.318
1966	ATL	158	603	168	44	127	.279
1967	ATL	155	600	184	39	109	.307
1968	ATL	160	606	174	29	86	.287
1969	ATL	147	547	164	44	97	.300

Key: MLN = Milwaukee Braves; ATL = Atlanta Braves; MIL = Milwaukee Brewers;
G = Games; AB = At-bats; H = Hits; HR = Home runs; RBI = Runs batted in;
BA = Batting average

☆ ☆ ☆ ☆ ☆ ☆

(continued)

YEAR	TEAM	G	AB	H	HR	RBI	BA
1970	ATL	150	516	154	38	118	.298
1971	ATL	139	495	162	47	118	.327
1972	ATL	129	449	119	34	77	.265
1973	ATL	120	392	118	40	96	.301
1974	ATL	112	340	91	20	69	.268
1975	MIL	137	465	109	12	60	.234
1976	MIL	85	271	62	10	35	.229
TOTALS		3,298	12,364	3,771	755	2,297	.305

Key: MLN = Milwaukee Braves; ATL = Atlanta Braves; MIL = Milwaukee Brewers; G = Games; AB = At-bats; H = Hits; HR = Home runs; RBI = Runs batted in; BA = Batting average

CHRONOLOGY

1934   **February 5** Born in Mobile, Alabama.

1951   Plays for the Mobile Black Bears, a local semiprofessional team.

1952   Receives contract to play for the Indianapolis Clowns; signed by the Boston Braves and sent to their farm team in Eau Claire, Wisconsin; wins the Rookie of the Year Award in the Northern League.

1953   Boston Braves move to Milwaukee; plays for the Jacksonville Tars in the South Atlantic League; wins the league's Most Valuable Player award.

1954   **April 13** Makes his major-league debut.

1955   Plays in his first All-Star Game.

1956   Wins the National League batting title, with a .328 average.

1957   **August 15** Hits his 100th career home run; Milwaukee Braves win National League pennant and defeat the Yankees to capture the World Series; named the National League Most Valuable Player.

1958   Wins his first Gold Glove; Braves again win National League pennant but fall to the Yankees in the World Series.

1959   Bats .355 to win his second National League batting title; wins his second Gold Glove.

1960   **July 3** Hits his 200th career home run; wins his third Gold Glove.

1963   **April 19** Hits his 300th career home run.

1965   Aaron and Eddie Mathews break record for the most home runs hit by two teammates.

1966   Milwaukee Braves move to Atlanta.

April 20 Hits his 400th career home run.

1968   **July 14** Hits his 500th career home run.

1970   **May 17** Hits a single for the 3,000th hit of his career.

1971   **April 27** Hits his 600th career home run.

1972   **June 10** Hits home run No. 649, moving into second place on the all-time home run list; breaks Stan Musial's record for total career bases.

1973   **July 21** Hits his 700th career home run.

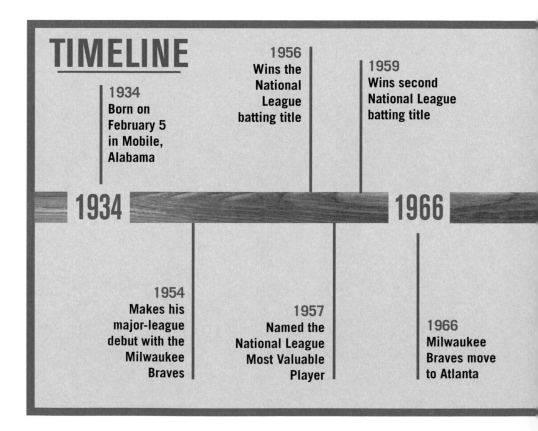

TIMELINE

1934
Born on February 5 in Mobile, Alabama

1956
Wins the National League batting title

1959
Wins second National League batting title

1934   1966

1954
Makes his major-league debut with the Milwaukee Braves

1957
Named the National League Most Valuable Player

1966
Milwaukee Braves move to Atlanta

1974   **April 4** Homers off Reds pitcher Jack Billingham at Riverfront Stadium to tie Babe Ruth's all-time home run record.

April 8 Hits home run No. 715 off Al Downing of the Los Angeles Dodgers, breaking Babe Ruth's major-league record.

November 2 Traded by the Atlanta Braves to the Milwaukee Brewers, where he will finish out his career.

1976   **October 3** Plays his final major-league game.

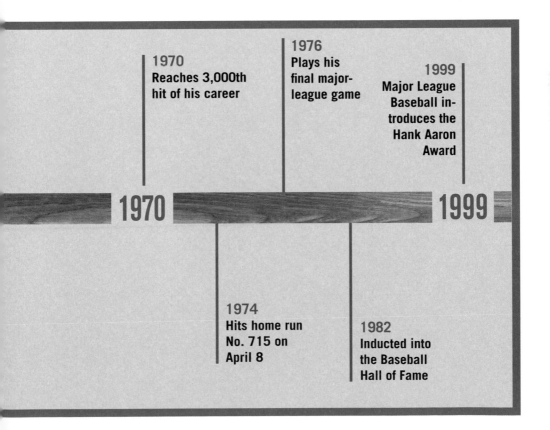

1970
Reaches 3,000th
hit of his career

1976
Plays his
final major-
league game

1999
Major League
Baseball in-
troduces the
Hank Aaron
Award

1970

1999

1974
Hits home run
No. 715 on
April 8

1982
Inducted into
the Baseball
Hall of Fame

1982   Inducted into the Baseball Hall of Fame.

1999   Major League Baseball introduces the Hank Aaron
Award for the best offensive players in each league;
named to baseball's All-Century Team; *Sporting News*
ranks Aaron No. 5 among 100 Greatest
Baseball Players.

2002   Receives Presidential Medal of Freedom.

GLOSSARY

at-bat (AB) An official turn at batting that is charged to a baseball player, except when the player walks, sacrifices, is hit by a pitched ball, or is interfered with by a catcher. At-bats are used to calculate a player's batting average and slugging percentage.

barnstorming To travel around the country appearing in exhibition sporting events.

batter's box The area to the left and right of home plate in which the batter must be standing for fair play to resume.

batting average A measure of the batting ability of a player, obtained by dividing the number of base hits by the number of official times at bat.

breaking ball Any pitch that markedly deviates from the "straight" or expected path because of a spin used by the pitcher; examples include the curveball, the slider, and the screwball.

cleanup The fourth position in the batting order, typically filled by the team's best home-run hitter.

curveball A pitch that curves on its way to the plate, thanks to the spin a pitcher places on the ball when throwing.

designated hitter In the American League, a player who bats each time for the pitcher. There is no designated hitter in the National League. Baseball is the only professional sport in which different rules apply in different sections of the league. The lack of consistency about the designated hitter is an ongoing debate.

doubleheader Two games played by the same two teams on the same day.

earned-run average (ERA) The average number of runs a pitcher allows per nine-inning game; the runs must be scored without errors by defensive players.

error   The game's scorer designates an error when a defensive player makes a mistake that results in a runner reaching base or advancing a base.

farm team   A team that provides training and experience for young players, with the expectation that successful players will move to the major leagues.

games behind   A statistic used in team standings. It is figured by adding the difference in wins between a trailing team and the leader to the difference in losses, and dividing by two. A team that is three games behind may trail by three in the win column and three in the loss column, or four and two, or any other combination of wins and losses totaling six.

Gold Glove   An award given to the most outstanding fielder at each position.

grand slam   A home run hit when the bases are loaded.

opposite-field hit   A hit to the "opposite" side of the field from the direction of a player's natural swing. For example, a left-handed hitter would hit to left field; a right-handed hitter, to right field.

pennant   The championship of each league in Major League Baseball.

pull   Hitting the ball to the inside portion of the field relative to the side of the plate on which the batter stands. (Right-handed batters pull the ball to the left side of the field; left-handed batters pull the ball to the right side of the field.)

roster   A list of people on a team.

runs batted in (RBI)   The number of runs that score as a direct result of a batter's hit(s) are the runs batted in by that batter. The major-league record is 191 RBIs in a single year by one batter.

screwball   A pitch that curves to the same side as the side from which it was thrown. For a right-handed pitcher, the ball would break to the right.

slider   A relatively fast pitch with a slight curve in the opposite direction of the throwing arm.

slugging percentage   The number of bases a player reaches divided by the number of at-bats. It is a measure of the power of a batter.

total bases   The number of bases reached by a batter as a result of base hits. A single = 1; a double = 2; a triple = 3; a home run = 4.

Triple Crown   A player wins the Triple Crown when he leads the league in batting average, home runs, and runs batted in at the end of a season.

BIBLIOGRAPHY

Aaron, Hank, with Wheeler, Lonnie. *I Had A Hammer: The Hank Aaron Story.* New York: HarperCollins, 1991.

Bolton, Todd. "History of the Negro Major Leagues." Negro League Baseball Players Association. Available online at *www.nlbpa.com/history.html.* Accessed August 2006.

"Hank Aaron." Baseball-Reference.com. Available online at *www.baseball-reference.com.* Accessed September 2006.

"Hank Aaron Detailed Biography." Net Glimse. Available online at *www.netglimse.com/celebs/pages/hank_aaron/index.shtml.* Accessed August 2006.

"Indianapolis Clowns." Negro League Baseball. Available online at *www.negroleaguebaseball.com/teams/Indianapolis_Clowns.html.* Accessed July 2006.

Johnson, Bruce "Charlie." "The Indianapolis Clowns: Clowns of Baseball." *The Clown in Times.* 6(3), 2000.

Ladson, William. "Q&A With Hank Aaron." *Sporting News,* April 8, 1999.

Naughton, Jim. "Hank Aaron, Beyond the Fences: From Slugger to Baseball Executive, Breaking Racial Barriers." *Washington Post,* June 29, 1987.

Plimpton, George. *One for the Record: The Inside Story of Hank Aaron's Chase for the Home-Run Record.* New York: Harper & Row, 1974.

Shatzkin, Mike. *The Ballplayers, Hank Aaron to Jim Lyttle: Baseball's Ultimate Biographical Reference.* New York: Idea Logical Press, 1990.

Stanton, Tom. *Hank Aaron and the Home Run That Changed America.* New York: HarperCollins Books, 2004.

Sykes, Tanisha A. "Power Hitter: Baseball Legend Hank Aaron Scores Big with His Import Dealerships." *Black Enterprise,* June 2004.

Yuhasz, Dennis. "Hank Aaron Biography." Baseball Almanac. Available online at *www.baseball-almanac.com/players/hank_aaron_biography.shtml.* Accessed August 2006.

FURTHER READING

Aaron, Hank, and Dick Schaap. *Home Run: My Life in Pictures.* Kingston, N.Y.: Total Sports Publishing, 1999.

Burns, Kenneth. *Baseball: An Illustrated History.* New York: Alfred A. Knopf, 1994.

Finlayson, Reggie. *We Shall Overcome: The History of the American Civil Rights Movement* (People's History). Minneapolis, Minn.: Lerner Publications, 2002.

Heward, Bill. *Some Are Called Clowns: A Season With the Last of the Great Barnstorming Baseball Teams.* New York: Crowell, 1974.

Kappes, Serena. *Hank Aaron* (Sports Heroes and Legends). Minneapolis, Minn.: Lerner Publications, 2005.

Margolies, Jacob. *The Negro Leagues: The Story of Black Baseball.* London: Franklin Watts, 1994.

Vascellaro, Charlie. *Hank Aaron: A Biography.* Westport, Conn.: Greenwood Press, 2005.

WEB SITES

Baseball Almanac

http://www.baseball-almanac.com/

Baseball Links

http://www.baseball-links.com/

Baseball Reference

http://www.baseball-reference.com

Historic Baseball

http://www.historicbaseball.com/

National Baseball Hall of Fame and Museum

http://www.baseballhalloffame.org

Negro League Baseball

http://www.negroleaguebaseball.com/

Negro League Baseball Players Association

http://www.nlbpa.com

Official Site of Major League Baseball

http://mlb.mlb.com/index.jsp

Sporting News: Hank Aaron Scrapbook

http://www.sportingnews.com/archives/aaron/index.html

Sports Illustrated—715: Hank Aaron's Glorious Ordeal

http://sportsillustrated.cnn.com/baseball/mlb/features/1999/aaron/aaron_story/

PICTURE CREDITS

INDEX

ABOUT THE AUTHOR

J. POOLOS has followed baseball closely for the past 34 years. He is the author of nine books of nonfiction for young readers and has written user guides for video games about baseball and other sports. He was 10 years old when he sat in front of the television and watched Hank Aaron hit his record-breaking home run.